Microsoft® FoxPro® For Windows™

Version 2.5

ONE 3.5"
DISK INCLUDED

Step by Step

Catapult

Microsoft PRESS

PUBLISHED BY
Microsoft Press
A Division of Microsoft Corporation
One Microsoft Way
Redmond, Washington 98052-6399

Library of Congress Cataloging-in-Publication Data
Microsoft FoxPro for Windows step by step / Catapult, Inc.
     p.   cm.
   Includes index.
   ISBN 1-55615-540-9
   1. Data base management.   2. Microsoft FoxPro for Windows.
 I. Catapult, Inc.
 QA76.9.D3M57 1993
 005.75'65--dc20   92-37695
                                 CIP

Printed and bound in the United States of America.

1 2 3 4 5 6 7 8 9 MLML 8 7 6 5 4 3

Distributed to the book trade in Canada by Macmillan of Canada, a division of Canada Publishing Corporation.

Distributed to the book trade outside the United States and Canada by Penguin Books Ltd.

Penguin Books Ltd., Harmondsworth, Middlesex, England
Penguin Books Australia Ltd., Ringwood, Victoria, Australia
Penguin Books N.Z. Ltd., 182-190 Wairau Road, Auckland 10, New Zealand

British Cataloging-in-Publication Data available.

The Catapult, Inc. Curriculum Development Group
Editor: Gregory G. Schultz
Authors: Marie L. Swanson and Daniel J. Swanson
Technical Editing: Bill Poole, Ph.D.

Contents

Part 1   Getting Started with Microsoft FoxPro for Windows

Part 2   Organizing Database Information

About This Book

Microsoft FoxPro for Windows is a powerful database management application that you can use for storing, organizing, and reporting the important information you need every day. *Microsoft FoxPro for Windows Step by Step* is a tutorial that shows you how to use FoxPro for Windows to simplify your work and increase your productivity. You can use this book in a classroom setting, or you can use it as a tutorial to learn FoxPro for Windows at your own pace and at your own convenience.

By completing the lessons in this book, you will learn how to use FoxPro for Windows to organize and manage database information that you now store in lists, card files, folders, and tables. This book also shows you how to use the powerful application development power tools in FoxPro for Windows to create your own custom applications with a minimum of programming.

Each lesson is designed to take an average of 30 to 45 minutes. You can set your own pace according to your personal learning style and experience level. Every lesson ends with a brief exercise, called "One Step Further." This part of the lesson builds on the skills you have learned so far and extends your understanding by introducing you to a new feature, a helpful option, or a shortcut technique to improve your productivity with FoxPro for Windows.

This book is divided into three major parts, each containing four lessons covering related skills and activities. At the end of each part, there is a Review & Practice scenario that gives you the opportunity to practice many of the skills you learned in that part. In this less-structured activity, you can test your knowledge and refine your skills before you go on to the next part of the book or work on your own.

Included with this book is a disk containing the files you need to get hands-on practice in the exercises. Instructions for copying the practice files to your computer's hard disk are in "Getting Ready," the next section in this book.

Finding the Best Starting Point for You

This book is designed for users learning FoxPro for Windows for the first time or for users who are familiar with FoxPro for DOS. Even if you are a novice user, *Microsoft FoxPro for Windows Step by Step* will help you to get the most out of FoxPro for Windows.

Each lesson builds on concepts presented in previous lessons, so it is a good idea to proceed through the lessons in consecutive order. The list at the start of each lesson identifies the skills and concepts you will learn.

Use the following table to determine your best first step.

If you are	Follow these steps
New to a computer or graphical environment, such as Microsoft Windows	Read "Getting Ready," the next section in this book. Follow the instructions for installing the practice files. Next, work through the lessons in order.
New to the mouse	Read "If You Are New to Using the Mouse" in "Getting Ready," the next section in this book. Follow the instructions for installing the practice files. Next, work through the lessons in order.
Familiar with a graphical environment and database management, but new to FoxPro for Windows	Follow the instructions for installing the practice files in "Getting Ready," the next section in this book. Next, work through the lessons in consecutive order.

Using This Book As a Classroom Aid

If you are an instructor, you can use *Microsoft FoxPro for Windows Step by Step* for teaching FoxPro for Windows to novice users. You may want to select certain lessons that meet your students' needs and incorporate your own demonstrations into the lessons.

If you plan to teach the entire contents of this book, you should probably set aside three full days of classroom time to allow for discussion, questions, and any customized practice you may create.

Conventions Used in This Book

Before you start any of the lessons, it is important that you understand the terms and notational conventions used in this book.

Notational Conventions

- Characters you are to type appear in **bold**.

- Important terms and titles of books appear in *italic*.

Procedural Conventions

- Procedures you are to follow are given in numbered lists (1, 2, and so on). A triangular bullet (▶) indicates a procedure with only one step.

- The word *choose* is used for carrying out an option.

- The word *select* is used for highlighting fields, text on a menu, and for selecting options in a dialog.

Mouse Conventions

- If you have a multiple-button mouse, it is assumed that you have configured the left mouse button as the primary mouse button. Any procedure that requires you to click the secondary button will refer to it as the right mouse button.

- *Click* means to point to an object and then press and release the mouse button. For example, "Click the text tool in the toolbox." The word *click* is used for selecting push buttons, radio buttons, and check boxes.

- *Drag* means to click and hold the mouse button while you move the mouse. For example, "Drag the field to the Group Footer band."

- *Double-click* means to rapidly press and release the mouse button twice. For example, "Double-click the FoxPro for Windows icon to start FoxPro for Windows."

  You can adjust the mouse tracking speed and double-click speed in Control Panel. For more information, see your system documentation.

Keyboard Conventions

- Names of keys are in small capital letters; for example, TAB and SHIFT.

- You can choose options with the keyboard. Press the ALT key to activate the menu bar, then press the keys that correspond to the underlined letters in the menu pad and the options. For some options, you can also press the key combination listed in the menu popup.

- A plus sign (+) between two key names means that you must press those keys at the same time. For example, "Press SHIFT+SPACEBAR" means that you hold down the SHIFT key while you press the SPACEBAR.

Other Features of This Book

Text tool

- You can perform many operations by clicking a tool in the toolbox. When a procedure instructs you to click a tool, a picture of the tool appears in the left margin of this book, as the text tool does here.

- Text in the left margin provides tips, additional useful information, or keyboard alternatives.

- The One Step Further exercise at the end of each lesson introduces new options that build on the features and skills you used in the lesson.

- The optional Review & Practice activity at the end of each major part provides an opportunity to use all of the skills presented in the lessons you have completed so far. These activities present problems that reinforce what you have learned and encourage you to recognize new ways in which you can use FoxPro for Windows.

Cross-References to FoxPro for Windows Documentation

References to the documentation that accompanies FoxPro for Windows software appear at the end of each lesson to acquaint you with other sources of information. These documents include:

- *Microsoft FoxPro for Windows Getting Started*
- *Microsoft FoxPro for Windows User's Guide*
- *Microsoft FoxPro for Windows Developer's Guide*
- *Microsoft FoxPro Language Reference*

Use these materials to take full advantage of the features in FoxPro for Windows.

Microsoft FoxPro for Windows Getting Started

This manual provides a brief overview of database management terms and concepts, plus hands-on demonstrations of FoxPro for Windows features and functions. Review this book to get a general idea of all the capabilities and power available in Microsoft FoxPro for Windows.

Microsoft FoxPro for Windows User's Guide

This extensive manual provides comprehensive information and detailed instructions for using all of the functions and options in FoxPro for Windows. Use it whenever you want more information about a particular topic covered in a lesson. It is organized to reflect the appearance and organization of the menus, options, and popups.

Microsoft FoxPro for Windows Developer's Guide

This manual provides all the information you need to create your own customized FoxPro for Windows applications. It includes an overview of the built-in power tools that make it easier to develop applications, as well as more advanced techniques for experienced programmers. Use this manual when you want to go beyond the basic application development topics covered in Part 3 of this book.

Microsoft FoxPro Language Reference

This manual provides a complete explanation of the FoxPro for Windows command language. Use this manual to get more information about specific commands available in the Command window. Commands and functions are organized by category in Section 1 and alphabetically in Section 2.

Online Help

FoxPro for Windows Help provides online information about FoxPro for Windows features and gives instructions for performing specific tasks. You will learn more about Help in "Getting Ready," the next section in this book.

Getting Ready

This section prepares you for your first steps into the FoxPro for Windows environment. You will review some useful Microsoft Windows techniques as well as terms and concepts important in your understanding of how to use FoxPro for Windows.

You will learn:

- How to install the practice files onto your computer hard disk.
- How to start Microsoft Windows.
- How to start FoxPro for Windows.
- About important features of the windows, menus, and dialogs in the FoxPro for Windows environment.
- How to use FoxPro for Windows Help.

Installing the Step by Step Practice Files

Included with this book is a disk called "Practice Files for FoxPro for Windows Step by Step." A special program on the disk automatically installs the practice files to your hard disk. These files are copied to a special PRACTICE directory created in the home directory where FoxPro for Windows is stored on your computer. The home directory is \FOXPROW.

Copy the practice files to your hard disk

1 Turn on your computer.

2 Insert the Practice Files disk into drive A.

3 At the MS-DOS command prompt (usually C:\), type **A:\INSTALL**

Do not type a space between "A:\" and "INSTALL."

4 Follow the instructions on the screen.

You can press CTRL + X at any time to exit the Step by Step setup program.

Using the Practice Files

As you work through the lessons using the practice files, be sure to follow the instructions for saving and giving the practice files a new name (except for the table files). Renaming the practice file allows you to make changes, experiment, and observe results, without affecting the original practice file. With the practice file intact, you can reuse the original file later if you want to repeat a lesson or try a new option.

Because the changes you make in tables take effect right away, you will not be able to repeat the activities in Lessons 1 and 2. To keep the original file intact, make of a copy of the CUSTOMER table before you begin. If you want to restore a table to its original state, you can also copy the duplicate files located in the BACKUPDB directory under PRACTICE.

Important

All Step by Step activities use and create files in the PRACTICE directory under FOXPROW. The Review & Practice activities use and create files in the REVIEW directory under PRACTICE. The active directory name always appears above the Directory list in the Open dialog. Be sure the correct directory is active before you open or save a file. To make a directory active, you double-click the directory name in the Directory list in the Open dialog. Simply selecting or highlighting a directory name does not make it the active directory.

Lesson Background

For these lessons, imagine that you are the PC Support person for Sweet Lil's, a manufacturer and distributor of gift chocolates. As Sweet Lil's operations expand, the company's information requirements also increase. Throughout these lessons, you use FoxPro for Windows to assist you in providing various departments at Sweet Lil's with the information they need to do their work.

The table below lists the names of the practice files you need to start each lesson. The table also identifies any files you create or save after you complete a lesson.

Lesson Files

Lesson	Practice files	Created or saved files
1	CUSTOMER.DBF CUSTOMER.FPT	NA
2	CUSTOMER.DBF CUSTOMER.FPT	NA
3	CUSTOMER.DBF CUSTOMER.FPT LSNQ03.QPR	CA1YEAR.QPR NESUBS.QPR NOTCA.QPR NY2YEAR.QPR

Lesson	Practice files	Created or saved files
4	LSNQ04.QPR OSFQ04.QPR	Q04NESUB.FRT Q04NESUB.FRX Q04NESUB.QPR SWEETQ04.FRT SWEETQ04.FRX SWEETQ04.QPR
5		BONBOX05.DBF
6	BONBONS.DBF BOX.DBF BOXES.DBF BOXES.FRT LSNQ06.QPR	SWEETQ06.FRT SWEETQ06.FRX SWEETQ06.QPR
7	ORDERS.DBF	ORDERSRT.CDX ORDERS.DBF
8	BONBONS.CDX BOX.CDX CUSTOMER.DBF CUSTOMER.FPT LSNR08MD.FRT LSNR08MD.FRX ORDER.DBF ORDERS.DBF ORDERS.FPT OSFR08.FRT OSFR08.FRX OSFV08.VUE	BOXES.CDX ORDER.CDX SWEET08.VUE
9	BONBONS.DBF LSNS09B.SCT LSNS09B.SCX	SWEET09A.SCX SWEET09A.SPR SWEET09B.SCX SWEET09B.SPR
10	BONBONS.DBF LSNS10A.SCT LSNS10A.SCX LSNS10B.SCT LSNS10B.SCX LSNS10C.SCT LSNS10C.SCX	BUTTON10.SCX BUTTON10.SPR SWEET10B.SCX SWEET10B.SPR SWEET10C.PJX SWEET10C.SCX SWEET10C.SPR

Lesson	Practice files	Created or saved files
11	ABOUTBOX.SCT ABOUTBOX.SCX APPMENU.MNT APPMENU.MNX BONBONS.DBF	
12	BONCHOC.QPR BONID.QPR BONNAME.QPR LSNR12.FRT LSNR12.FRX RBONCHOC.QPR RBONID.QPR RBONNAME.QPR SWEET10C.PJX	SWEET12.PJX

Review & Practice Files

Part	Practice files	Created or saved files
1	EMPLOYEE.DBF EMPLOYEE.FPT	REVQ01.FRX REVQ01.QPR
2	EQUIPMNT.DBF INVENTRY.DBF	EMPLOYEE.CDX EQUIPMNT.CDX INVENTRY.CDX REVQ02.FRX REVQ02.QPR REVT01.DBF REVT02.DBF
3	EMPLOYEE.DBF REVQDEPT.QPR REVQEMPL.QPR	APPMENU.MNT APPMENU.MNX REVS03.PJX REVS03.SCX REVS03.SPR

Starting an Application

After you install FoxPro for Windows and copy the practice files, you can start the application.

Starting Microsoft Windows

Use the following procedure to start Microsoft Windows. Your screen may be different from the illustrations in this book, depending on your particular setup and the applications installed on your computer. For more information about Windows, see the *Microsoft Windows User's Guide*.

Start Windows from the MS-DOS command prompt

1   At the system prompt, type **win**

2   Press ENTER.

You can start all of your applications, including FoxPro for Windows, from Program Manager.

When Windows is active, everything on your screen (called the *desktop*) is displayed in a *window*. You can adjust each window to the size you want and you can move windows anywhere you want on the desktop. You can have multiple windows open at the same time to compare and share information easily.

Within the Program window are symbols that represent applications and documents. These symbols, called *icons,* are used to open the applications they represent. The icons are organized in groups, usually related to applications. The default installation of FoxPro for Windows creates a group named FoxPro. You use these icons to open the applications they represent.

As you become more familiar with Windows, you will find that you can customize the startup screen to your personal working style.

Starting FoxPro for Windows

Double-clicking the FoxPro for Windows group icon opens the FoxPro for Windows program group window. This window contains the icons for FoxPro for Windows and its related applications.

Start FoxPro for Windows

1   Double-click the FoxPro for Windows group icon.

    This opens the FoxPro for Windows program group.

2   Double-click the FoxPro for Windows program icon.

FoxPro for
Windows

If You Are New to Microsoft Windows

For new Microsoft Windows users, this section provides a general overview of what you can accomplish within this graphical environment. Windows is designed for both ease of use and sophistication of function. It helps you handle virtually all of the daily work that you carry out with your computer. Microsoft Windows provides a common basis among different application programs—both in the way they share data and in the way you control their operations.

Once you become familiar with the basic elements of Microsoft Windows, you can apply these skills to learn and use FoxPro for Windows, as well as many other types of applications, including word processing, graphics, and spreadsheets.

Using Microsoft Windows Applications

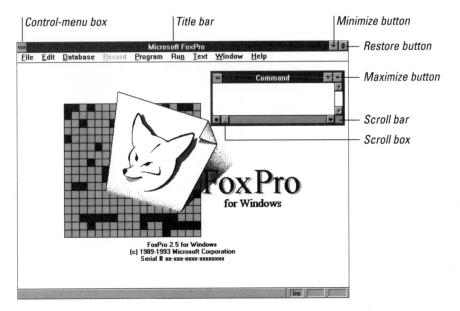

You can scroll, move, split, and close a window by using the mouse.

To	Do this
Scroll through a window (to see another part of the project)	Click the scroll bars, or drag the scroll box.
Enlarge a window to fill the screen	Double-click the title bar, or click the Maximize button.
Shrink a document window to an icon in the FoxPro for Windows workspace	Click the Minimize button.
Restore a window to its previous size	Click the Restore button.
Move a window	Drag the title bar.
Close a window	Double-click the Control-menu box.

Using Help

FoxPro for Windows Help is a complete online reference. You can get Help information in several ways.

To get Help information	Do this
By topics or by activity	From the Help menu, choose Contents.
While working in a dialog	Press F1.

Display the list of Help topics

▶ From the Help menu, choose Contents.

The Help Table of Contents window looks like the following illustration.

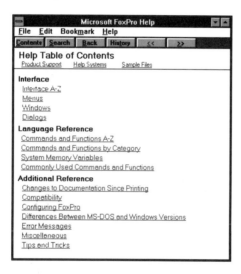

Clicking an underlined term "jumps" you to a related topic. Clicking the Back push button in the Help window returns you to the previous help topic.

Clicking a term with a dotted underline displays a popup topic in a topic window. This window provides a definition or presents you with other topics to which you can jump.

You can size, move, and scroll through a Help window. You can switch between the Help window and the FoxPro for Windows application, or you can arrange the windows side by side so that you can refer to Help while you work.

Getting Help on Help

To learn how you can make the best use of all the information in Help, choose the How To Use Help option from the Help menu.

Learn to use Help

1 From the Help menu, choose How To Use Help.

The Contents For How To Use Help window looks like the following illustration.

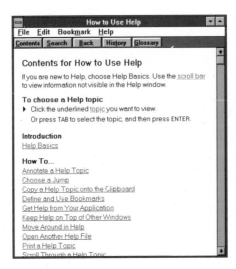

2 Click the word "topic," which has a dotted underline.

3 Click anywhere in the window to remove the popup topic.

4 Under How To, click the underlined text, Print A Help Topic.

The Help window for Printing A Help Topic looks like the following illustration.

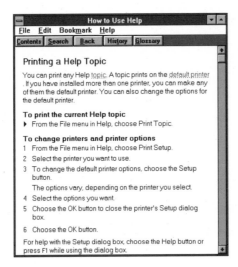

5 Click the Contents push button to return to the Contents For How To Use Help window.

6 From the File menu, choose Exit.

Getting Help on a Specific Topic

The Search option allows you to quickly locate help topics by using one or more key words. If you know the command or term you want help on, you can go directly to the topic.

Search for a topic

1 Press F1 to display the Help window.

This selection is the same as choosing Search For Help On from the Help menu.

2 Click the Search push button.

3 In the Search dialog, type **view window**

These are the key words that will be searched for. The View Window topic appears in the list.

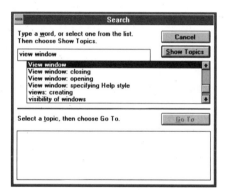

4 Choose the Show Topics push button.

5 When the View Window topic appears in the bottom of the Search dialog, click the Go To push button.

The View Window topic window appears.

Note   You will use the View window throughout this book. Read this help topic now to familiarize yourself with its features.

---

6 After you are done, double-click the Control-menu box in the upper-left corner of the Help window to close Help and return to the FoxPro for Windows application window.

Getting Familiar with the FoxPro for Windows Environment

There are two ways to use FoxPro for Windows. You can enter commands in the Command window, or you can use the menus and dialogs to perform the operations you want. The first method reflects the early history of database software, before graphical environments, when database users were often developers and programmers. The second method reflects the latest innovations in software usability. For users new to computer software, and database software in particular, using menus and dialogs provides easy access to all of the most powerful FoxPro for Windows features without requiring you to memorize commands.

Although most of the activities in this book focus on using the menus and dialogs, there are many opportunities to use the Command window.

Using FoxPro for Windows

FoxPro for Windows uses different kinds of windows so that you can do a variety of tasks. You can have many windows open at one time, and you can minimize, maximize, restore, and move these windows around on your desktop. Working with multiple windows means you can quickly get to the task you want to do next by simply activating (that is, clicking) the window you want. Here is a quick overview of the windows you use most in FoxPro for Windows.

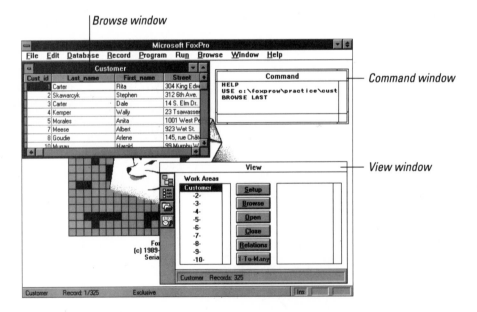

Browse window — Command window — View window

Browse window   This window lets you view the contents of a database in a format of rows and columns. In FoxPro for Windows, *table* refers to the file in which database information is stored.

View window   In this window, you can open, browse, close, set up, and set relations in multiple work areas. A *work area* is the area in which you work with a table. You can have only one table open in a work area at one time. If you want to work with several tables at once, you can use the View window to open another table in another work area.

Command window   In this window, you can type the FoxPro for Windows command to perform the operation you want. Because of the great number of programmers and developers already using earlier versions of FoxPro, this method is still available to anyone who wants to invest the time and energy to learn literally hundreds of FoxPro for Windows commands. In some cases, the Command window provides additional features and extra flexibility. All of the commands are described in detail in the *Microsoft FoxPro Language Reference*.

You work in other windows when you use the FoxPro for Windows power tools: the Report Writer, the Screen Builder, the Application Generator, the Menu Builder, and Project Manager. For a complete overview of the windows and power tools you use in FoxPro for Windows, see *Microsoft FoxPro for Windows Getting Started*.

Using FoxPro for Windows Menu Popups and Options

For those who prefer the intuitive Microsoft Windows environment, the menus and dialog boxes (called *dialogs* in FoxPro for Windows) provide virtually the same features and functions found in the Command window. If you are familiar with other Microsoft Windows applications, you will notice some minor differences in the terminology of FoxPro for Windows. This book uses FoxPro for Windows terminology so that you can look up information in the FoxPro for Windows documentation and online Help.

In FoxPro for Windows, menus and commands perform according to Microsoft Windows conventions. Menu names (called *menu pads*) appear in the *menu bar*, across the top of the screen. A list (called a *menu popup*) of commands (called *options*) appears when you click a menu pad. To choose an option, click the menu pad to open the menu popup, and select an option.

When you need to supply information for an option to be carried out, a dialog appears on the screen. After you enter information or make selections in the dialog, click the OK push button with the mouse, or press the ENTER key to carry out the option. Choose the Cancel push button, or press ESC to close a dialog and cancel.

The following illustration shows the FoxPro for Windows menu bar with the Edit menu popup displayed.

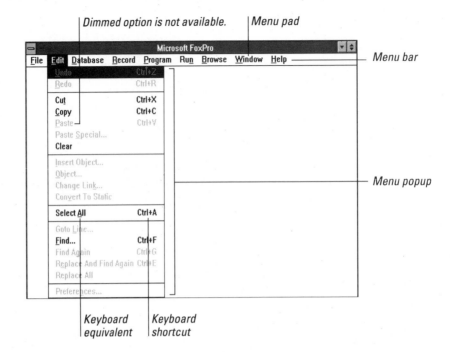

Some options have a *keyboard shortcut* combination listed to the right of the option name. Once you are familiar with the menus and options, these keyboard shortcuts can save you time.

In addition, most options have keyboard equivalents. If you are not using a mouse, you make selections by pressing ALT and the underlined character of the menu pad. To select an option from a menu popup, you can simply type the underlined character when the menu popup is displayed.

When an option name appears dimmed, it does not apply to your current situation or is unavailable. For example, the Paste option on the Edit Menu popup appears dimmed if the Copy option or Cut option has not been used first.

The list of options on a menu popup can change depending on the type of window that is active.

When an option name displays a check mark to its left, the option is already in effect.

Snap To Grid is in effect.

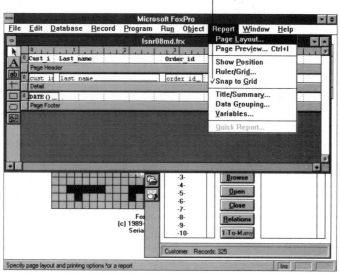

To close a menu popup without choosing an option, click the menu pad again.

Using Dialogs

When you choose an option name that is followed by an ellipsis (. . .), a dialog appears so that you can provide more information. Depending on the dialog, you type the information, or you choose from a group of options.

For example, the Font dialog is displayed when you choose the Font option from the Text menu. In the dialog, you specify the characteristics you want. The Font dialog looks like the following illustration.

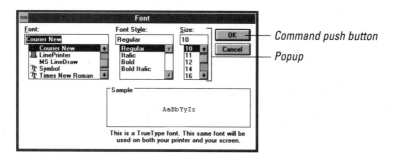

Every dialog has at least one or more of the following items (called *controls*) to help you supply the information necessary to carry out the option.

Command push button   You choose a command push button to carry out an operation or to display more options. If a push button is dimmed, it is unavailable. An ellipsis following the name of a command push button means that more options are available. Choose the OK push button to carry out an operation, or choose the Cancel push button to cancel.

Text box   You type information in a text box. For example, in the Font box you can type the name of the font you want.

List   Available choices are presented in a list. If the list is longer than the box, you can use the scroll bar to see the rest of the list.

Popup   You can choose an option from a popup. This kind of control requires you to click a down arrow that is next to the control to see a list of choices.

Radio buttons   You can select only one option at a time from a group of radio buttons. A selected radio button has a black dot in its center.

Check boxes   You select check boxes to choose options that can be combined with one another, so you can select more than one at a time. In FoxPro for Windows, some check boxes are followed by ellipses; check boxes display a dialog when you click them.

Selecting Dialog Options

To move around in a dialog, click the item you want. You can also hold down ALT and press the key for the underlined letter at the same time. Or, you can press TAB to move between items.

Use the procedures in this table to select options in a dialog with the mouse.

To	Do this
Select or clear a radio button	Click the radio button.
Select or clear a check box	Click the check box.
Select an item in a list	Click the item.
Move to a text box	Click the text box.
Select text in a text box	Double-click a word, or drag over the characters.
Select all text in a text box	Triple-click a word, or press CTRL+A.
Scroll through a list	Use the scroll bars.

Using Toolboxes

Line tool

In the Report Layout window and Screen Design window, you use tools to create and move objects. These tools are grouped in a toolbox at the left edge of the window. For example, to create a line in a report, you click the line tool and the pointer changes shape. After you position the pointer in the Report Layout window, you drag the pointer to create the line you want.

If You Are New to Using the Mouse

Toolboxes, menus, and many other features of FoxPro for Windows were designed for working with the mouse. Although you can use the keyboard for most actions in FoxPro for Windows, many of these actions are easier to do with the mouse.

Mouse Pointers

The mouse controls a pointer on the screen. You move the pointer by sliding the mouse over a flat surface in the direction you want the pointer to move. If you run out of room to move the mouse, lift it up and put it down again. The pointer moves only when the mouse is touching the flat surface.

Moving the mouse pointer across the screen does not affect the document; the pointer simply indicates a location on the screen. When you press the mouse button, something happens at the location of the pointer.

When the mouse pointer passes over different parts of the FoxPro for Windows window, it changes shape, indicating what it will do at that point. Most of your work in this book will use the following mouse pointers.

This pointer	Appears when you point to
⌖	The menu bar and toolboxes to choose a command or a button, the title bar to move a window, or the scroll bars to scroll through a document.
↔	A column-heading boundary to change column width or a row-heading boundary to change row height.
⋪⋫	The window splitter on the scroll bar to split a window vertically.
☝	A button on a worksheet, or a term in a Help topic that you can click to go to another topic.
I	Text in a text box. When you click the mouse in a text box, the pointer is called an *insertion point*.

Using the Mouse

These are the four basic mouse actions that you use throughout the lessons in this book.

Pointing   Moving the mouse to place the pointer on an item.

Clicking   Pointing to an item on your screen and then quickly pressing and releasing the mouse button. You select items on the screen and move around in a document by clicking.

Double-clicking   Pointing to an item and then quickly pressing and releasing the mouse button twice. This is a convenient shortcut for many tasks in FoxPro for Windows.

Dragging   Holding down the mouse button as you move the pointer. You can use this technique to select data in the rows and columns in tables.

Quitting FoxPro for Windows

▶ From the File menu, choose Exit.

You can also double-click the Control-menu box in the upper left corner of the application window.

Warning   Because each window has a Control-menu box that you can double-click, be careful to note which window you are closing, especially when you only want to close a window without leaving FoxPro for Windows.

Quitting Microsoft Windows

If you would like to quit, here is a simple way to exit the program and Microsoft Windows.

Quit Microsoft Windows

1   Hold down the ALT key, and press F4.

2   When you see a box with the message "This will end your Windows session," press ENTER.

Getting Started with Microsoft FoxPro for Windows

Looking at Your Information

The Browse window allows you to examine, enter, and modify database information in a table. In this lesson, you will open a table and use the Browse window to view information in the table. Then you will make changes to the Browse window to rearrange how the information is displayed. Finally, you will enter information in fields.

You will learn how to:

- Open a table.

- Browse through a table.

- Move around in the Browse window.

- Modify the Browse window.

- Make entries in fields.

Estimated lesson time: 40 minutes

Double-clicking the FoxPro for Windows group icon opens the FoxPro for Windows program group window. This window contains the icons for FoxPro for Windows and its related applications.

Start FoxPro for Windows

1 Double-click the FoxPro for Windows group icon.

This opens the FoxPro for Windows program group.

2 Double-click the FoxPro for Windows program icon.

FoxPro for
Windows

Understanding Databases

Databases are everywhere: Telephone directories, recipe files, and catalogs are all examples of databases. Any information that can be used as a list or that is stored as a collection of forms or cards is a database. Computer-based databases (the kind that FoxPro for Windows enables you to create and use) are simply faster, more flexible, and often larger versions of their paper-based counterparts. In fact, when a paper-based database gets too large to maintain or use reliably, using database management software like FoxPro for Windows is the answer.

Getting Information from Forms

Using a completed new customer card as an example, you can get an idea of where database data comes from. Here is a new customer subscription form, indicating that this new customer wants to receive Sweet Lil's monthly magazine, *The Chocolate Gourmet*.

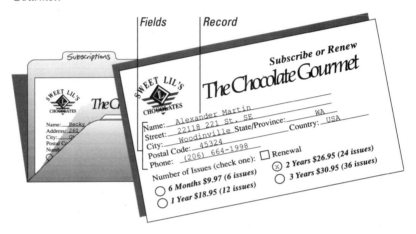

Each blank on this card represents a *field*. A field is a single piece of data of a particular type. For example, "Name" and "Number of Issues" are fields. All of the fields on this card form the *record* for this customer. A record is a collection of related fields. All of the records for all the customers subscribing to *The Chocolate Gourmet* constitutes a database of Sweet Lil's subscribers. Information about these customers might be maintained by a circulation department, used in a billing department, and summarized and organized for a marketing department. By having all this database information stored in a FoxPro for Windows *table*, it is easy to keep track of all the information that is important.

Note   In FoxPro for Windows, a file in which database information is stored is called a *table*.

Opening a Table

To see the contents of a table, you must open the table and then view the contents in the Browse window. There are several ways to do this, but the most convenient method is to use the View option from the Window menu.

In the View window you can open, browse, close, set up, and set relations in multiple work areas. A *work area* is the area in which you work with and use a table. You can have only one table open in one work area at a time. If you want to work with several tables at once, you can use the View window to open another table in another work area. In Lesson 8, you will learn how to work in multiple work areas.

Open the CUSTOMER table

1 From the Window menu, choose View.

The View window appears. Work Area 1 is selected.

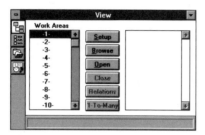

2 Click the Open push button.

The Open dialog appears.

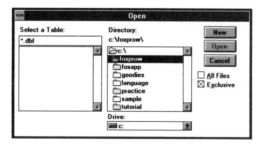

3 In the Directory list, double-click the PRACTICE directory.

PRACTICE is now the current directory. Its path appears above the Directory list.

4 In the Select A Table list, select the table called CUSTOMER.DBF.

5 Click the Open push button.

The CUSTOMER table is now open in Work Area 1 and stays open until you close it.

Browsing Through a Table

After you open a table, you can display its contents in the Browse window. Using the Browse window, you can view your data, change the data, add and delete entries, and search for specific entries. For now, open the Browse window, and examine the data in the CUSTOMER table.

Open the Browse window

▶ In the View window, click the Browse push button.

Your screen looks like the following illustration.

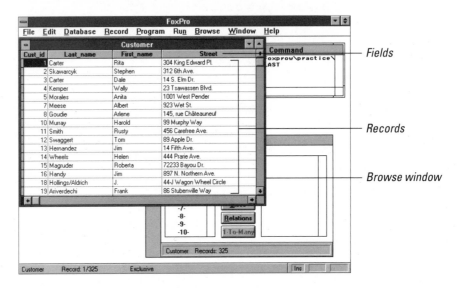

The CUSTOMER table contains information for over 300 customers. All of the information related to a specific customer is one record. In the Browse window, each row represents a record.

Understanding Fields in Tables

The individual pieces of data about a customer (such as name, address, city, and state) are *fields*. Notice that the field names at the top of each column in the Browse window correspond roughly to the fields on the subscription form. Not all of the fields come from the form; for example, the Sub_date field is provided by the Circulation department when they process a subscription request. Even though the Browse window currently displays only a few fields at a time, there are actually 13 fields for each customer in the CUSTOMER table.

Each record in a table can contain as many as 255 fields or as few as one field. In the Browse window, each column represents a field.

Fields can contain different types of information, such as:

- Dates

- Numbers, which can be used in calculations

- Logical values, which indicate whether something is true or false

- Text

The field type determines the kind of data the field can contain. For example, date fields contain dates, numeric fields contain numbers, logical fields contain a true/false value, and character and memo fields contain text. Memo fields differ from other fields in that you cannot examine their contents simply by looking at the field in the Browse window. Later in this lesson, you will learn how to open memo fields, examine their contents, and enter information in them. In Lesson 5, you will learn more about the other types of fields as you create your own table.

Moving Around in the Browse Window

By scrolling horizontally, you can see the other fields in a record. By scrolling vertically, you can see the other customer records.

See other fields

1   Click the right arrow at the right corner of the horizontal scroll bar.

The Browse window moves one field to the right.

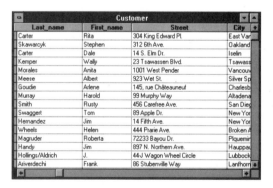

2   Click to the right of the scroll box in the horizontal scroll bar.

The Browse window moves several fields to the right.

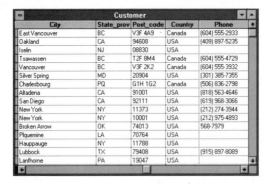

3   Click the left arrow at the left corner of the horizontal scroll bar.

The Browse window moves one field to the left.

4   Click to the left of the scroll box in the horizontal scroll bar.

The Browse window moves several fields to the left.

See other records

1   Click the down arrow at the bottom of the vertical scroll bar.

The Browse window moves downward one record in the table.

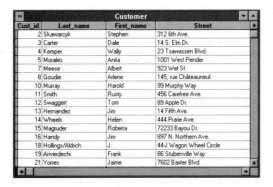

2   Click below the scroll box in the vertical scroll bar.

The Browse window moves downward one screen of records in the table.

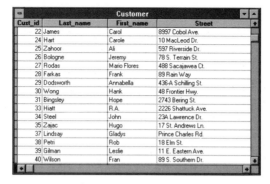

3   Click the up arrow at the top of the vertical scroll bar.

The Browse window moves up one record in the table.

4   Click above the scroll box in the vertical scroll bar.

The Browse window moves up one screen of records in the table.

Modifying the Browse Window

To see more (or less) information at one time, you adjust the size of the Browse window to make it larger or smaller. You can also split the Browse window into two partitions so that you are viewing different parts of the table at the same time.

Adjust the size of the Browse window

1   Move the pointer to the right edge of the Browse window.

2   When the pointer changes to a white two-headed arrow, drag it to the right.

The Browse window becomes wider, revealing more fields in the table.

3   Move the pointer to the right edge of the Browse window.

4   When the pointer changes to a white two-headed arrow, drag it to the left.

The Browse window becomes narrower, revealing fewer fields in the table.

5   Move the pointer to the bottom edge of the Browse window.

6   When the pointer changes to a white two-headed arrow, drag it downward.

The Browse window becomes taller, revealing more records in the table.

Adjust the width and length at the same time

1   Move the pointer to the bottom right corner of the Browse window.

2   When the pointer changes to a white two-headed arrow, drag it downward and to the right.

The Browse window becomes larger, revealing more records and fields in the table.

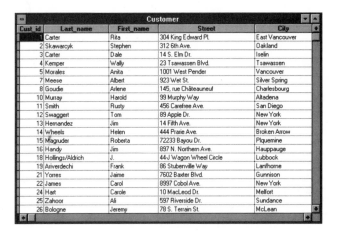

Partitioning the Browse Window

As you scroll in the Browse window, you might observe that it can be difficult to keep track of which record you are working on. For example, you want to know when customer 254 started subscribing to *The Chocolate Gourmet.* You can see the Cust_id field, but not the date field. If you scroll right to the Sub_date field, you no longer see the Cust_id field and cannot determine which start date belongs to this customer.

By dragging the window splitter to the right, you *partition* the Browse window, splitting the window into two parts. The window splitter is located at the lower left corner of the Browse window. Because you can scroll in each of the partitions, you can arrange the fields so that the left partition displays the Cust_id field and the right partition displays the Sub_date field.

Partition the Browse window

▶ Drag the window splitter at the lower left corner of the Browse window to the middle of the window.

Position the pointer here, and drag it.

A second vertical scroll bar divides the Browse window into two partitions as shown in the following illustration.

Change the active partition

Now the right partition is active. This means that any operation you perform occurs in the right partition. To change the active partition, click in any field in the left partition.

1 Click a field in the left partition.

The left partition is now active.

2 Drag the vertical scroll box for the left partition about halfway down until you see customer ID 254.

3 Click to the right of the scroll box in the horizontal scroll bar for the left partition.

The left partition scrolls to the right; the fields displayed in the right partition remain unchanged.

4 Drag the horizontal scroll box all the way to the left until the Cust_id field displays.

5 In the right partition, click the Cust_id field for customer ID 254.

6   Drag the horizontal scroll box for the right partition to the right until the Sub_date field displays.

Now you can see both of the fields you need at the same time as shown in the following illustration.

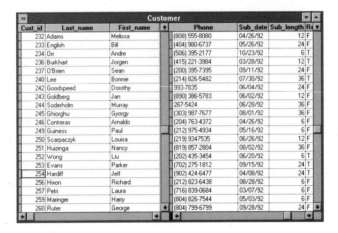

Unlink partitions

After you first partition the Browse window, the partitions are *linked*. This means that if you scroll vertically in one partition, the records in the other partition scroll the same number of records in the same direction you scrolled. By unlinking the partitions, you can scroll vertically in each partition without affecting what is displayed in the other.

This technique lets you look at different parts of the table at the same time. Before you start, scroll the right partition all the way to the left so that both partitions display the Cust_id field.

1   From the Browse menu, choose Link Partitions.

This removes the check mark from the Link Partitions option, unlinking the two partitions.

2   Drag the vertical scroll box for the right partition to about one quarter of the way up the vertical scroll bar.

The records in the right partition move up, while the records in the left partition remain unchanged as shown in the following illustration.

Partitions scroll independently.

Link partitions

1 From the <u>B</u>rowse menu, choose <u>L</u>ink Partitions.

This adds a check mark in front of the Link Partitions option, linking the two partitions. In addition, the left partition positions itself to display the same records shown in the right partition.

2 Drag the vertical scroll box for the left partition to about halfway down the vertical scroll bar.

Records in both partitions scroll downward simultaneously.

Remove the Browse window partition

▶ Drag the window splitter at the bottom of the partition to the left edge of the Browse window.

The partition between the two windows disappears.

Working with Browse Window Fields

Not only can you change the size and partitions of the Browse window, you can adjust the size of individual fields to make them larger or smaller. You can arrange the fields in the Browse window so that only those fields you want to see are displayed. You can also enter and modify information displayed in any field.

Change the size of a field

1 Scroll to the Country field.

2 Move the pointer near the right edge of the Country field heading.

3   When the pointer changes to a black two-headed arrow, drag it to the left. Use the following illustration to give you an idea of how wide to make the field.

The fields to the right of the adjusted field move to the left in the Browse window.

Position the pointer here.

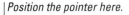

Customer		
st_code	**Country**	**Phone**
829	USA	993-7835
718	USA	(890) 386-5783
274	USA	267-5424

Drag the pointer to about here.

City	State_prov	Post_code	Country	Phone	Sub_date	Sub_le
Escanaba	MI	49829	USA	993-7835	06/04/92	
Black Hawk	SD	57718	USA	(890) 386-5783	06/02/92	
Pinckneyville	IL	62274	USA	267-5424	06/28/92	
Durango	CO	81301	USA	(303) 987-7677	08/01/92	
Shilo	MB	R0K 2A0	Canada	(204) 763-4372	04/26/92	
Brooklyn	NY	11211	USA	(212) 975-4934	05/16/92	
Fort Wayne	IN	46816	USA	(219) 9347535	06/26/92	
Eskimo Point	NT	X0C 0E0	Canada	(819) 857-2804	08/02/92	
Washington	DC	20008	USA	(202) 435-3454	06/20/92	
Las Vegas	NV	89114	USA	(702) 275-1812	09/15/92	
Kingston	NS	B0P 1R0	Canada	(902) 424-6477	04/08/92	
New York	NY	10016	USA	(212) 823-6438	08/28/92	
Buffalo	NY	14202	USA	(716) 839-0684	03/07/92	
Newport News	VA	23604	USA	(804) 826-7544	05/03/92	
Newport News	VA	23607	USA	(804) 799-6799	09/28/92	
Charleston	WV	25301	USA	(304) 975-6946	09/19/92	
Montague	PE	C0A 1R0	Canada	(902) 838-3356	07/02/92	
Frankfort	KY	40601	USA	(502) 948-9685	05/28/92	
Fargo	ND	58103	USA	(701) 546-5467	05/05/92	
Freemont	CA	94538	USA	(414) 796-9799	07/01/92	
Tallahassee	FL	32303	USA	(904) 973-9573	05/19/92	

Rearrange fields in the Browse window

Suppose you want to focus on the customer first name, last name, and phone number. You can rearrange the fields so that these three fields are displayed together in the Browse window. By rearranging the fields in the Browse window, you can minimize the amount of horizontal scrolling you have to do to see the fields you use the most.

1   Drag the heading of the First_name field to the left so that it appears before the Cust_id field.

2   Drag the heading of the Last_name field to the left so that it appears after the First_name field.

3   Scroll to the right until you see the Phone field.

4   Drag the heading of the Phone field so that it appears after the Last_name field.

The Browse window looks like the following illustration.

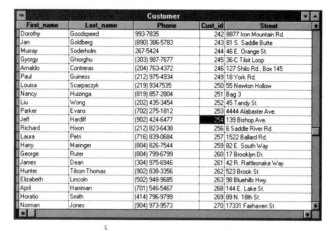

First_name	Last_name	Phone	Cust_id	Street
Dorothy	Goodspeed	993-7835	242	8877 Iron Mountain Rd.
Jan	Goldberg	(890) 386-5783	243	81 S. Saddle Butte
Murray	Soderholm	267-5424	244	46 E. Orange St.
Gyorgy	Ghiorghu	(303) 987-7677	245	36-C Tilsit Loop
Arnaldo	Contreras	(204) 763-4372	246	127 Shilo Rd., Box 145
Paul	Guiness	(212) 975-4934	249	18 York Rd.
Louisa	Scarpaczyk	(219) 9347535	250	55 Newton Hollow
Nancy	Huizinga	(819) 857-2804	251	Bag 3
Liu	Wong	(202) 435-3454	252	45 Tandy St.
Parker	Evans	(702) 275-1812	253	4444 Alabaster Ave.
Jeff	Hardiff	(902) 424-6477	254	139 Bishop Ave.
Richard	Hixon	(212) 823-6438	256	6 Saddle River Rd.
Laura	Petri	(716) 839-0684	257	1522 Ballard Rd.
Harry	Maringer	(804) 826-7544	259	82 E. South Way
George	Ruter	(804) 799-6799	260	17 Brooklyn Dr.
James	Dean	(304) 975-6946	261	42 R. Rattlesnake Way
Hunter	Tilson-Thomas	(902) 838-3356	262	523 Brook St.
Elizabeth	Lincoln	(502) 948-9685	263	98 Bluehills Hwy.
April	Harriman	(701) 546-5467	268	144 E. Lake St.
Horatio	Smith	(414) 796-9799	269	89 N. 18th St.
Norman	Jones	(904) 973-9573	270	17331 Fairhaven St.

Note   You are changing only the *arrangement* of the fields displayed in the Browse window. You are not affecting the structure or the organization of the information stored in the table.

Making Entries in a Field

You can do more in the Browse window than simply look at and rearrange your information. You can also enter and modify information displayed in any field.

In most cases, you can change the contents of a field by selecting and editing the field. For example, you can change a last name by selecting the field containing an individual's name and typing in a new name.

Change a customer name

1   Click the Last_name field for customer ID 220.

2   Position the insertion point at the end of the existing text in the field by pressing END.

3   Type **-Smith**

The data in the table is now updated to Hamstrung-Smith.

Working with Memo Fields

To enter information in a memo field, you must open it first. You can tell at a glance if there already is information in a memo field. If the field displays the word "memo" with a lowercase "m," it means that the field is empty; if the field displays the word "Memo" with an uppercase "M," it means that the field contains text.

When you first look at a memo field, you see only the word "memo" or "Memo." You need to open a memo field before you can see its contents. To open a memo field (whether or not it contains an entry), you double-click the word "memo." When it is open, you can edit the contents by typing over, inserting, or deleting text in it.

Because memo fields can contain almost an infinite amount of free-form text, they are useful for descriptions, comments, and other information that are not easily categorized.

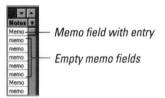 — *Memo field with entry*

— *Empty memo fields*

Find a memo field with information

1   To keep track of the record on which you are working, drag the window splitter to the right of the Cust_id field.

2   In the left partition, scroll vertically to customer ID 202.

3   Click the Cust_id field for this customer.

4   In the right partition, scroll horizontally to the Notes field for this customer.

Open the memo field

▶   Double-click the memo field to open it.

The contents of the memo field appears in a memo field window for this customer.

Contents of the memo field

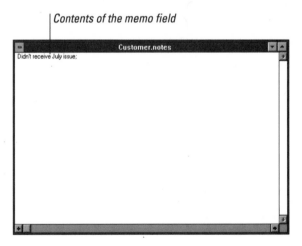

Edit the memo field

1   Place the insertion point after the semicolon, and type **re-sent on 8/2/92** in the memo editing window.

2   Double-click the Control-menu box to close the memo editing window.

Double-click here.

Find an empty memo field

▶   Scroll vertically through the left partition to customer ID 101.

This memo field displays the word "memo" in lowercase because it currently contains no information.

Tip   Click the Cust_id field before scrolling in the left partition. Clicking a field "fixes" the horizontal position of the left partition.

Open the memo field

▶   Double-click the memo field to open it.

Make an entry in the memo editing window

1   Type **Bonus subscription** in the memo editing window.

2   Double-click the Control-menu box to close the memo editing window.

The memo field for this customer now displays the word "Memo," indicating it contains information.

One Step Further

When several records have similar information in the same fields, you can use some simple editing techniques to save time and prevent typographical errors. You can copy the contents of one memo field and then paste the contents into any memo field for which the same information applies.

For example, the Customer Service department has informed you that several customers did not receive the bonus box of candy as promised. After ensuring that another box is sent, go to a record that contains a note to this effect, copy the text, and then paste the text in the other records.

Copy the contents of a memo field

1   Open the memo field for customer ID 382.

You can also triple-click to select an entire field.

2   Select all the text by pressing CTRL+A.

3   From the Edit menu, choose Copy.

4   Double-click the Control-menu box to close the memo editing window.

5   Open the memo field for customer ID 282.

6   From the Edit menu, choose Paste.

7   Double-click the Control-menu box to close the memo editing window.

If You Want to Continue to the Next Lesson

1   From the Window menu, choose View.

2   In the View window, click the Close push button.

If You Want to Quit FoxPro for Windows for Now

▶   From the File menu, choose Exit.

Lesson Summary

To	Do this
Open a table	From the Window menu, choose View. Then click the Open push button. From the Open dialog, double-click the directory and table name.
Open the Browse window, (if your table is already open)	From the Browse menu, choose Browse.
Move one field to the right in the Browse window	Click the right arrow on the horizontal scroll bar.
Move several fields to the right	Click to the right of the scroll box in the horizontal scroll bar.
Move downward one record in a table	Click the down arrow at the bottom of the vertical scroll bar.
Move downward several records in a table	Click below the scroll box in the vertical scroll bar.
Move up one record in a table	Click the up arrow at the top of the vertical scroll bar.

To	Do this
Move up several records in a table	Click above the scroll box in the vertical scroll bar.
Make the Browse window wider	Drag the right edge of the Browse window to the right.
Make the Browse window narrower	Drag the right edge of the Browse window to the left.
Make the Browse window taller	Drag the bottom edge of the Browse window downward.
Adjust the width and length at the same time	Drag the bottom right corner of the Browse window downward and to the right.
Partition the Browse window	Drag the window splitter at the bottom left corner of the Browse window to the center of the window.
Change the active partition	Click anywhere in the partition that you want to activate.
Unlink partitions	From the Browse menu, choose Link Partitions. (Removes check mark from option.)
Link partitions	From the Browse menu, choose Link Partitions. (Places a check mark in front of the option.)
Remove the Browse window partition	Drag the window splitter at the bottom of the partition to the left corner of the Browse window.
Change the size of a field	Drag the right edge of the field heading to the left or to the right.
Rearrange fields in the Browse window	Drag the field title to the new position.
Enter or edit information in a memo field	Double-click the word "memo" to open the memo field. Insert, type over, or delete text in the memo editing window.

For more information on	See in *Microsoft FoxPro for Windows Getting Started*
Menus, dialogs, and windows	Chapter 3, Groundwork
Opening and browsing a database	Chapter 3, Groundwork
Modifying the Browse window	Chapter 3, Groundwork
Working in a Memo window	Chapter 4, Looking at Your Data

For more information on	See in the *Microsoft FoxPro for Windows User's Guide*
Menus, dialogs, and windows	Chapter 1, Interface Basics
Editing text	Chapter 3, Edit Menu
View windows and work areas	Chapter 7, Window Menu

Preview of the Next Lesson

In the next lesson, you will learn how to maintain the information in your table by entering new records, removing unnecessary records, and changing information in individual records.

Working with Records

All the information about a specific entry in your table is stored in a record. Maintaining the information in your table means entering new records, removing records you no longer need, and changing the information in a record. In this lesson, you will learn two different ways to locate a record, and you will learn how to use the Browse window and Change window in FoxPro for Windows to keep your table up to date.

You will learn how to:

- Add a record.
- Locate a record with selection criteria.
- Jump to a specific record.
- Delete a record.
- Undo an entry.
- Modify information in the Change window.

Estimated lesson time: 35 minutes

If you closed FoxPro for Windows at the end of the last lesson

▶ Double-click the FoxPro for Windows icon to start FoxPro for Windows.

Open the CUSTOMER table

1   In the Window menu, choose View.

2   In the View window, click the Open push button.

3   In the Directory list, double-click PRACTICE to make it the current directory.

   PRACTICE is already the current directory if you did not exit FoxPro for Windows at the end of the last lesson.

4   In the Select A Table list, select the table called CUSTOMER.DBF.

5   Click the Open push button.

Adding New Records

As you saw in Lesson 1, you can use the Browse window to examine and edit information in a table. In the Browse window, you can also add new records to a table. For example, a stack of mail-in subscription forms represents new customers who need to be added to the CUSTOMER table. To add a new customer's information, you must open the Browse window. You can open the Browse window from either the View window or the Command window.

Open the Browse window from the View window

When you open the Browse window from the View window, the Browse window appears as it looked the last time you used it. The arrangement of fields, any partitioning, or any linking is still in effect from the previous lesson.

▶ In the View window, click the Browse push button.

The Browse window looks like the following illustration.

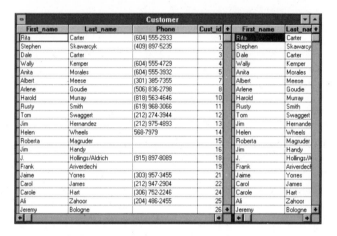

Open the Browse window from the Command window

As described in Getting Ready, the commands displayed in the Command window usually correspond to the options you choose from the menus. Occasionally, however, there are slight differences. The last line of text in the Command window now reads "BROWSE LAST." This command causes the Browse window to assume its previous settings and appearance. You can restore the Browse window to its default settings (using the arrangement of fields found in the table, without any partitioning or linking) by using the Browse command in the Command window.

1 From the Window menu, choose Command.

2 In the Command window, type **browse** at the insertion point.

3 Press ENTER.

The Browse window returns to its default setting.

Cust_id	Last_name	First_name	Street
1	Carter	Rita	304 King Edward Pl.
2	Skawarcyk	Stephen	312 6th Ave.
3	Carter	Dale	14 S. Elm Dr.
4	Kemper	Wally	23 Tsawassen Blvd.
5	Morales	Anita	1001 West Pender
7	Meese	Albert	923 Wet St.
8	Goudie	Arlene	145, rue Châteauneuf
10	Murray	Harold	99 Murphy Way
11	Smith	Rusty	456 Carefree Ave.
12	Swaggert	Tom	89 Apple Dr.
13	Hernandez	Jim	14 Fifth Ave.
14	Wheels	Helen	444 Prarie Ave.
15	Magruder	Roberta	72233 Bayou Dr.
16	Handy	Jim	897 N. Northern Ave.
18	Hollings/Aldrich	J.	44-J Wagon Wheel Circle
19	Ariverdechi	Frank	86 Stubenville Way

Add a new record

Add this customer to the CUSTOMER table.

1 From the Browse menu, choose Append Record.

    The Browse window scrolls down to the first blank row.

2 In the Cust_id field, type **437**

3 Press TAB to move from one field to the next as you enter the following information.

4 In the Last_name field, type **Grussman**

5 In the First_name field, type **Steve**

6 In the Street field, type **183 Orchard Lane**

7 In the City field, type **Appleton**

8 In the State_prov field, type **WI**

9 In the Post_code field, type **54911**

10   In the Country field, type **USA**

11   In the Phone field, type **(414) 831-2228**

12   In the Sub_date field, type **12/12/92**

Do not type the slashes when you enter a date.

13   In the Sub_length field, type **6**

14   In the Renewal field, type **F**

When you are in the
last field of a record,
you can also press
TAB to move to the
first field. Pressing
SHIFT+TAB moves you
to the last field when
you are in the first
field of a record.

15   Click to the left of the scroll box in the horizontal scroll bar until the first field, Cust_id, appears in the Browse window.

Your Browse window now looks like the following illustration.

│ New record

Locating a Record

When one of the CUSTOMER records was first entered, the handwriting on the subscription form for the customer was unclear, so it was difficult to see the correct city. You entered "Fort Myer" but added some question marks after the city name. Now that you have verified the name of the city, you need to locate this customer record so you can correct it.

So far, we have been locating a record by referring to a value in one of its fields, as in "Move to the record for customer ID 202." You would then scroll through the table to find that record. Fortunately, there is a more convenient way to locate and move directly to a specific record in a table. Using the Locate option and the Expression Builder, you can specify the field and its contents for the record you want to find.

The Expression Builder is a dialog in which you enter *expressions*. Expressions are fields, often combined with operators and selection criteria, that you specify when you want to limit the results of an option. For example, you want the Locate option to find only those records that contain the text "Fort Myer??" You need to enter an expression that determines which records the Locate option should find. The Expression Builder makes it easy to create the expression you need.

When FoxPro for Windows finds the first record that matches your selection criteria, it positions the pointer in the first field in that record. If there are more records that match, you can tell FoxPro for Windows to go to the next matching record.

Locate a record with Expression Builder

Use the Locate option and the Expression Builder to locate the record containing "Fort Myer??" in the City field.

1   From the Record menu, choose Locate.

The Locate dialog appears. Currently, the Scope box indicates that you want to include all the records in the table in your search for matching records.

Click here.

2   Click the For push button.

With the For and While push buttons, you can specify a range of records to include in the search. Unlike the Scope option, this range is specified in terms of the information found in specified fields, rather than in a number of records.

The Expression Builder dialog appears.

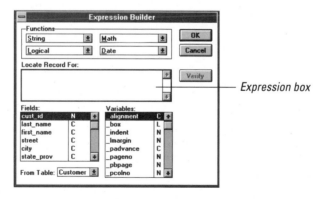

Expression box

The name for the expression box reflects the kind of operation you are doing.

3   In the Fields list, double-click City.

The dialog displays the field you select (with the insertion point) in the expression box preceded by the table name.

4 Type the equal sign (=) after the field name.

5 In the Functions area, click the String popup, and then click "text."

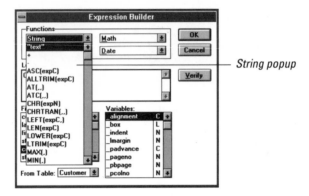

A set of quotation marks appears in the Locate Record For box. The insertion point is positioned between them. This selection means that the field you want to locate contains text (rather than numbers that you can use in a calculation or a true/false setting).

6 In the Locate Record For box, type **Fort Myer??**

7 Click the Verify push button.

The status bar displays a message indicating the expression is valid. When you click the Verify push button, FoxPro for Windows checks to make sure that you have entered field names found in the table and that you have provided all the information needed to perform the option.

8 Click the OK push button to return to the Locate dialog.

In the Locate dialog, the For box contains the field expression you built in the Expression Builder dialog, or as much of the field expression that fits in the box. Because you are not going to further define the range of records to search, leave the While box blank. With the While box blank, FoxPro for Windows searches for matching records until it reaches the end of the file.

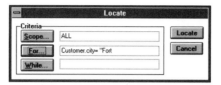

9 Click the Locate push button.

FoxPro for Windows moves to customer number 213, the record that matches the criteria you entered.

Edit the record

1 Move the pointer to the City field, and press END.

2 Press BACKSPACE twice to delete the two question marks from the entry, and type **s** to correct the city name.

Jumping to a Record

The number of the record on which you are working appears in the status bar at the bottom of the screen. The record number indicates the sequence in which the records were first entered in the table. It is different from the customer ID, which represents an internal record keeping system for Sweet Lil's. At first, the record number and the customer ID match one for one in the table. Later, as customers are deleted and added to the table, the record numbers and customer IDs no longer correspond directly. Nevertheless, knowing the record number provides a useful way to move to a specific record.

The status bar also displays the total number of records in the table.

Using the Goto option on the Browse menu (the option is also on the Record menu), you can enter the number of the record to which you want to go. For example, if you know that the record you want to see is number 88, you can use the Goto option and specify that record number. FoxPro for Windows then displays that record.

Go to a record

You want to verify the customer information that is located in record number 23. Use the Goto option to move directly to that customer record.

1   From the Browse window, choose Goto.

2   In the Goto dialog, click the Record radio button.

Click here.

3   In the Record box, type **23**

4   Click the Goto push button.

Record number 23 displays, and the status bar indicates you are in record 23.

Deleting Records

Adding new records is only one part of what you need to do to maintain your table. You also need to delete unnecessary records from the table. Deleting a record is actually a two-step process. First you *mark* a record for deletion, and then you *pack* the table to remove all the marked records. In this way, you can mark many records for deletion and use the Pack option to remove them all at once.

The Customer Service department has reported that several customers have canceled their subscriptions to *The Chocolate Gourmet*. You need to remove these customers from your CUSTOMER table. To do this, you mark the records for these customers. Later, you can pack the table to remove these records permanently.

Mark a record for deletion

Use the Goto option to move directly to the records you want to mark. Then mark the records.

1   Move to record number 316.

2   Click in the gray area to the left of the Cust_id field.

Deletion bar

The area to the left of the record is now shaded black (depending on the kind of monitor you are using), indicating it is marked for deletion.

A record marked for deletion

Alternatively, with the pointer in the record you want to mark, choose <u>T</u>oggle Delete from the Browse menu. This is the same as clicking in the gray area to the left of the field. Or, choose <u>D</u>elete from the <u>R</u>ecord menu. With this option, you can use the Expression Builder to delete a group of records that match a specified criteria.

3 Mark record numbers 217, 230, and 270 for deletion.

Changing Your Mind

Remember, the records you marked have not been removed yet. If you change your mind and decide that you do not want to delete a particular record, you can simply unmark the record.

You have just realized that you did not mean to mark Ms. Beauregard in Quebec, customer ID 272. Unmark this record so it is not deleted when you pack the table.

Unmark a record

1 Move to record number 217.

The customer ID is 272.

2 Click the area to the left of the Cust_id field.

The area to the left of the record is no longer black, so the record is not marked for deletion.

Packing the Table

When you are ready to permanently remove the marked records from the table, you can use the Pack option. Once a table is packed, you cannot restore any records marked for deletion. If you are certain that you no longer want these customers in your CUSTOMER table, use the Pack option to remove them.

Pack the table

1 From the <u>D</u>atabase menu, choose <u>P</u>ack.

2 Choose the Yes push button in the confirmation dialog.

FoxPro for Windows removes these records from the table and closes the Browse window.

3 In the View window, click the Browse push button.

The records for the customers you marked are now removed from the table. You can scroll through the Browse window and see that the records for these customers are no longer there. Also notice that the record numbers following the first record you deleted are reordered: The customer IDs remain the same, but the record numbers have changed.

Working in the Change Window

So far in these lessons, you have been using the Browse window for working in your table. The Browse window row-and-column format makes it easy to see information about many records at one time, and it can be helpful when you want to review more of your table at once. However, when you want to focus on all the information for just one record, you might prefer to use the Change window.

You can use the Change window to perform all the operations you learned to use in the Browse window. But instead of displaying information in rows and columns, the Change window displays all the fields for one record in a single column.

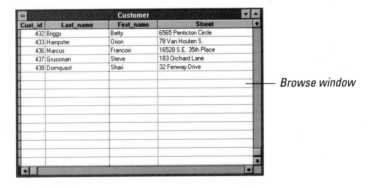

— Browse window

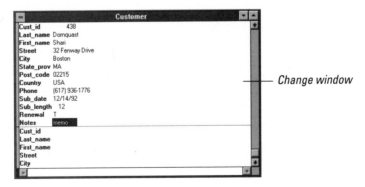

— Change window

Open the Change window

▶ From the Browse menu, choose Change.

Add a new record

Add another customer to the table.

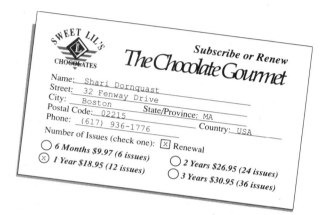

1   From the Record menu, choose Append.

The Change window scrolls down to the first blank record.

2   In the Cust_id field, type **438**

3   Press TAB to move to the Last_name field, and type **Dornquast**

4   Press TAB to move from one field to the next as you enter the following information.

5   In the First_name field, type **Shari**

6   In the Street field, type **32 Fenway Drive**

7   In the City field, type **Boston**

8   In the State_prov field, type **MA**

9   In the Post_code field, type **02215**

10   In the Country field, type **USA**

11   In the Phone field, type **(617) 936-1776**

12   In the Sub_date field, type **12/14/92**

13   In the Sub_length field, type **12**

14   In the Renewal field, type **t**

Your Change window looks like the following illustration.

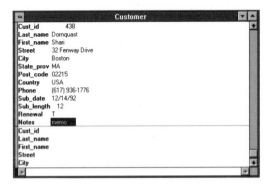

Modify a record in the Change window

You just realized that you made a mistake while entering information for a customer you added earlier in this lesson. Move to record number 323, and make the following changes.

1   Scroll to record number 323.

The customer ID is 437.

2   In the Street field, place the insertion point before the word "Lane."

3   Type **View** and a space.

4   Press TAB to move to the next field.

5   Return to the Street field, and select the word "Lane" by dragging across it.

6   Press DELETE to remove the word from the address.

Using Undo

After you make an entry, but before you move to another field, you can undo what you just entered by choosing the Undo option from the Edit menu. The Undo option eliminates the results of only the last operation.

In the previous step, you deleted a word from the address. Now you discover that "Lane" is also part of the address. Correct this mistake with the Undo option.

Undo an entry

You can also press CTRL+U to undo the previous operation.

▶   From the Edit menu, choose Undo.

"Lane" is restored to the address, but "View" is not removed, because you cannot undo an editing operation after you press TAB or otherwise move to a new field.

Return to the Browse window

▶   From the Browse menu, choose Browse.

One Step Further

The Replace option is a great way to correct mistakes made consistently throughout a table. For example, an intern has mistakenly entered Wisconsin as "Wisc." instead of "WI" in many of the State_prov fields. Instead of using the Locate option to find each record and make each correction individually, you can use the Replace option to make all the corrections at one time. Use your understanding of using the Expression Builder to specify the field you want to locate, the contents of the field, and what you want to replace the current contents with.

1 From the Record menu, choose Replace.

2 In the field name list, select State_prov.

3 Click the Scope check box.

4 In the Scope dialog, click the All radio button, and then click the OK push button.

5 Click the For check box to display the Expression Builder dialog, so you can specify the current field contents.

6 Double-click State_prov in the Fields list.

7 Type an equal sign (=) after the field name, and then type **"Wisc."**

Tip   Surrounding your text with quotation marks gives the same result as selecting "text" from the String popup, and then entering your text. You can use the method with which you are most comfortable.

---

8 Click the OK push button.

9 Click the With push button to display the Expression Builder dialog, and then specify the new field contents.

10 With the insertion point in the WITH box, type **"WI"**

11 Click the OK push button.

12 Click the Replace push button.

If You Want to Continue to the Next Lesson

1 From the Window menu, choose View.

2 In the View window, click the Close push button.

If You Want to Quit FoxPro for Windows for Now

▶ From the File menu, choose Exit.

Lesson Summary

To	Do this
Add a new record	From the Browse menu, choose Append Record.
Delete records	First *mark* a record for deletion, and then use the Pack option to remove all marked records.
Mark a record for deletion	Click in the area to the left of the first field in the record.
Pack the table	From the Database menu, choose Pack.
Unmark a record	Click in the area to the left of the first field in the record.
Open the Change window	From the Browse menu, choose Change.
Undo an entry	Before you move to another field, from the Edit menu, choose Undo. *or* Press CTRL+U to undo the previous operation.

For more information on	See in *Microsoft FoxPro for Windows Getting Started*
Adding records	Chapter 10, Working with Your Own Table (Entering Data in a Table)

For more information on	See in the *Microsoft FoxPro for Windows User's Guide*
Working with records	Chapter 5, Record Menu

For more information on	See in the *Microsoft FoxPro for Windows Language Reference*
Using the Command window	Overview of the FoxPro Language
Browse command	Browse
Browse Last command	Browse Last

Preview of the Next Lesson

In the next lesson, you will learn how to retrieve only the information you need. With the RQBE feature of FoxPro for Windows, you can create a query that will search for the information you specify and display it for you.

Retrieving Your Information

After information is in a table, you might want to retrieve the information and display only the fields and records you need. With the Relational Query By Example (RQBE) feature in FoxPro for Windows, you can create a query to search for and then display records based on selection criteria you specify.

In this lesson, you will learn how to open the RQBE window and do a query. After you use the Browse window to examine the information found with the query, you will create your own query by specifying the fields you want to include or exclude. You will also learn how to make changes and prioritize selection conditions so that you get just the information you want. Finally, you will establish the order in which the fields are sorted in a query.

You will learn how to:

- Open a query.
- Do a query.
- Create a query.
- Remove fields.
- Order fields.
- Specify selection conditions.
- Save a query.
- Modify a query.
- Prioritize selection conditions.
- Order by multiple fields.

Estimated lesson time: 35 minutes

If you closed FoxPro for Windows at the end of the last lesson

▶ Start FoxPro for Windows by double-clicking the FoxPro for Windows icon.

Open the CUSTOMER table

1 From the Window menu, choose View.

2 In the View window, click the Open push button.

3   In the Directory list, double-click PRACTICE to make it the current directory.

PRACTICE is already the current directory if you did not exit FoxPro for Windows at the end of the last lesson.

4   In the Select A Table list, select the table called CUSTOMER.DBF.

5   Click the Open push button.

Retrieving Data with Queries

In the previous lesson, you worked with all the records in the entire table in the Browse window. Queries, on the other hand, allow you to see a subset of the table: records that are temporarily extracted according to criteria you specify. By using queries, you can focus on only those records you need at the moment.

For example, if you want to see only your California customers, you can create a query that displays only records of the customers in California. Although you could use the Locate option to find these records one at a time, queries have the added benefit of allowing you to save your selection criteria, so you can reuse the query whenever you want to display these specific records. A query also lets you specify which fields you want displayed for the selected records, allowing you to further customize the display of information you want.

Sweet Lil's Marketing department wants to know which customers have renewed their subscriptions to Sweet Lil's monthly magazine, *The Chocolate Gourmet*. To find only these customers, use a query that has already been created for this purpose.

Open a query

Queries are stored in query files on your computer hard disk. Query files have the QPR extension. You use the Open option on the File menu to open the query you want to use. When you open a query, the details of the query appear in the RQBE window.

1   From the File menu, choose Open.

The Open dialog appears.

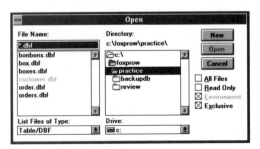

2   In the List Files Of Type popup, select Query.

3   In the File Name list, select LSNQ03.QPR.

This query has been created for this exercise and is provided on the exercise disk supplied with this book.

4   Click the Open push button.

The details of the query appear in the RQBE window. From the RQBE window you can create, modify, and run queries.

Understanding the RQBE Window

Different parts of the RQBE window allow you to specify a number of characteristics about your query.

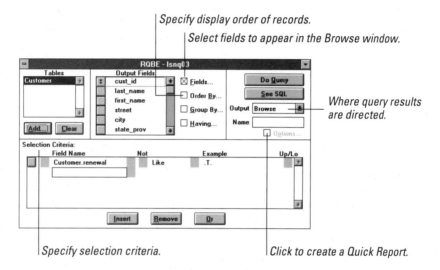

Specify display order of records.

Select fields to appear in the Browse window.

Where query results are directed.

Specify selection criteria.

Click to create a Quick Report.

Output Fields   In this area, you specify the fields you want displayed in the Browse window. You click the Fields check box to display the RQBE Select Fields dialog in which you select the fields you want. The fields you select appear in the Output Fields list area. In the LSNQ03.QPR query, all the available fields are included for each selected record.

Order By   This check box allows you to specify how you want the selected records sorted.

Output   In this popup, you can specify where you want the results of the query to go. For example, query results can go to the Browse window, a report, a label, or to another file. In this query, output is directed to the Browse window; this is the default selection.

Options   Select the Options check box to indicate how you want the selected records displayed. When you click this check box the RQBE Option dialog appears. In this dialog, you can access the Quick Report dialog, which lets you arrange output fields in rows or in columns. In this query, this selection is not used.

Selection Criteria   In this area of the RQBE window, you enter the selection criteria you want the selected records to match. For a record to match the criterion in this query, the Customer.renewal field must contain a "T." You will learn more about specifying selection criteria and using comparison operators later in this lesson when you create your own query.

Do a query

▶ Click the Do Query push button in the upper-right corner of the dialog.

The Browse window displays only those records that contain "T" in the Renewal field.

Notice the message in the status bar. It tells you how many records match your selection criteria.

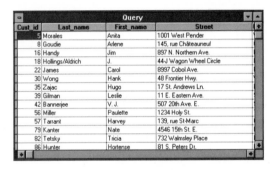

This Browse window operates much like the Browse window you used in the previous lesson, with one important exception: You cannot modify the records displayed in the Browse window as the result of a query. Scroll through the Browse window to examine these records.

Close the Browse window

▶ Double-click the Control-menu box to close the Browse window.

Close the RQBE window

▶ Double-click the Control-menu box in the RQBE window.

Important   Be careful not to double-click the Control-menu box on the application window—this will exit you from FoxPro for Windows.

Creating Your Own Query

You need to examine the records for those customers who have two-year (or longer) subscriptions and live in New York state. In this exercise, you create a query that displays the customer records for only these customers.

Select Work Area 1

▶ In the View window, choose Customer in Work Area 1.

Open the RQBE window

Use the New option on the File menu to create the query you want. When you specify that you want to create a query, FoxPro for Windows displays the RQBE window.

1 From the File menu, choose New.

The New dialog appears.

2 Click the Query radio button.

3 Click the New push button.

The RQBE window appears.

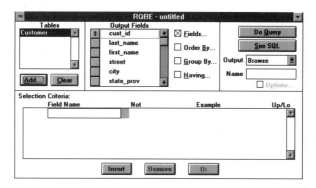

Specifying Output Fields

In the LSNQ03 query, the Browse window displayed all the fields for each record that matched the selection criteria in the query. In the query you are creating, you want to focus on the fields important to you right now. The RQBE window allows you to specify that the selected records display only the fields you want.

Open the RQBE Select Fields dialog

▶ Click the Fields check box.

Click here.

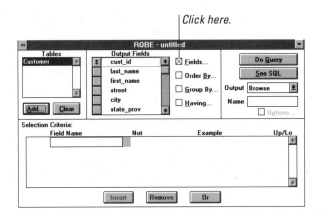

You must click the check box (even if it is already selected) to display the RQBE Select Fields dialog.

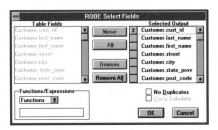

The field names displayed in the Selected Output list on the right side of the dialog are the output fields for this query. FoxPro for Windows automatically lists all the fields as output fields.

Removing Fields from a Query

In this query, you do not want to see all the fields in the Browse window. In fact, you want to see only the last name, the first name, the customer ID, renewal, subscription date, and length of subscription for each customer.

Remove some of the fields from the Selected Output list on the right side of the dialog to display the fields you want.

Remove fields one at a time

1   In the Selected Output list, select Customer.street.

The Remove push button is enabled.

2   Click the Remove push button to remove this field from the list.

3   In the Selected Output list, double-click Customer.city.

Double-clicking a field name in the Selected Output list also removes the field from the list.

4   In the Selected Output list, double-click Customer.notes.

Remove multiple fields

1   In the Selected Output list, select Customer.state_prov.

2   Scroll down the list until you see Customer.phone.

You can press the CTRL key while you click to select fields that are not next to each other in the list.

3   Hold down the SHIFT key, and click Customer.phone.

All the fields between and including Customer.state_prov and Customer.phone are selected.

4   Click the Remove push button to remove all these fields at once.

Ordering Output Fields

When you run this query, the fields you specified will be displayed for each record in the Browse window. They will be displayed in the order indicated in the Selected Output list. However, by dragging the Mover button for individual fields (the button to the left of the field name), you can position the fields where you want them.

Mover buttons

Because you are most interested in seeing the customer ID followed by the customer name, renewal, subscription length, and the subscription date, you need to reorder the fields so that they are displayed in the order you want.

Arrange fields

1   Drag the Mover button for the Customer.renewal field so that it appears after the Customer.first_name field.

2   Drag the Mover button for the Customer.sub_length field so that it appears after the Customer.renewal field in the list.

The list of fields in the Selected Output list looks like the following illustration.

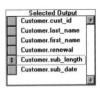

3   Click the OK push button to return to the RQBE window.

Specifying Selection Criteria

Now that you have indicated what fields to display for selected records in the Browse window, you need to specify the criteria to use to select the records themselves. The Selection Criteria area of the RQBE window makes it easy to select the records you want to see.

In the Field Name popup, you select a field that you want included in your selection criteria. In the comparison operator popup, you identify how you want the field to be compared to what you enter in the Example box. This table summarizes the comparison operators from which you can choose.

Comparison operator	Description
Like	The field in the record must match the Example column, ignoring upper/lowercase and extra spaces.
Exactly Like	The field in the record must match the Example column, *exactly*. This means the case, as well as any extra spaces, must match what is in the Example box.
More Than	The field in the record must be greater than the amount in the Example box. Values that are equal to the example are not to be selected.
Less Than	The field in the record must be less than the amount in the Example box. Values that are equal to the example box are not to be selected.
Between	The field in the record must be within the range of values in the Example box. Values that are equal to the start or end of the range are not to be selected.
In	The field in this record must match at least one of the items listed in the Example box.

In this query, you will specify the records for those customers living in New York state (NY) who have two-year or longer subscriptions (more than 23 months). To do this, specify that NY should appear in the State_prov field. Then specify that the subscription length field (Sub_length) should be more than 23 months.

Note   You can specify selection criteria for fields that are not included in the list of output fields.

Enter selection criteria

To enter selection criteria, you select fields from the Field Name popup, and then enter the values you want the fields to contain in the Example box.

1   In the Selection Criteria area of the RQBE window, click the blank box under Field Name.

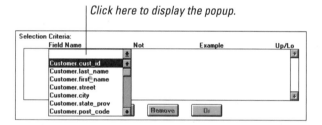

Click here to display the popup.

2   From the Field Name popup, select the Customer.state_prov field.

3   Press TAB two times to move to the comparison operator list.

The Like comparison operator is already selected. You do not need to change this field.

4   Press TAB again to move to the Example box.

5   Type **NY**

6   Click the blank box under Field Name.

7   From the Field Name popup, select the Customer.sub_length field.

8   Press TAB two times to move to the comparison operator popup.

9   Click the down arrow to the right of the popup and select More Than.

10   Press TAB once to move to the Example box.

11   Type **23**

The More Than and the Less Than comparison operators are not inclusive. This means you must use example data that includes all the data you want. In this case, use 23 to include two years (24 months) or more.

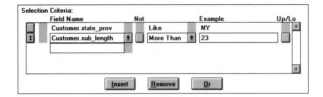

Do the query

▶ Click the Do Query push button.

The Browse window displays only those records that contain NY in the Customer.state_prov field and more than 23 in the Sub_length field. Scroll through the Browse window to examine these records.

Note   Because you know all the selected records contain NY in the State_prov field, you do not need to display this field. Including this field as one of the output fields would display information you already know because you specified this requirement in the query.

Your query now looks like the following illustration.

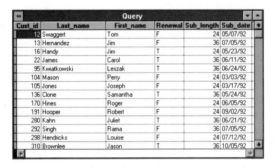

Close the Browse window

▶ Double-click the Control-menu box in the Browse window.

Saving a Query

You can save this query on your hard disk so you can re-use it whenever you want to examine these records. There are two ways to save a query: With the RQBE window open, choose the Save option from the File menu and enter a name for your query file; or, you can save your query file when you close the RQBE window and are asked to save the query.

Save a query file

Save your query file by closing the RQBE window.

1   Double-click the Control-menu box to close the RQBE window.

2   Click the Yes push button when you see the message about saving changes to UNTITLED.QPR.

The Save As dialog appears.

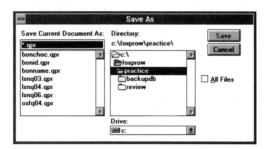

3   In the Save Current Document As box, type **NY2YEAR**

FoxPro for Windows provides the QPR extension.

4   Click the Save push button to close the dialog.

Modifying a Query

You can modify a saved query when your information needs to change. In fact, it can often take a few attempts to get the information you need. For example, Sweet Lil's Marketing department ran a promotion in the August issue for New York state subscribers. They want to find out how successfully the promotion encouraged new, longer (more than two years) subscriptions. After you see the results of this query, you will modify the query so that it displays exactly the information you want.

Instead of creating a new query from scratch, you can make changes to an existing query that already has many of the elements you want. The NY2YEAR query currently specifies customers living in New York state who have a two-year or longer subscription. Add a third selection criterion to select records with a subscription date after 9/21/92.

Open the RQBE window

1   From the File menu, choose Open.

The Open dialog appears.

2   In the File Name list, select NY2YEAR.QPR.

In the List Files Of Type popup, be sure Query is still selected.

3 Click the Open push button.

The details of the query appear in the RQBE window.

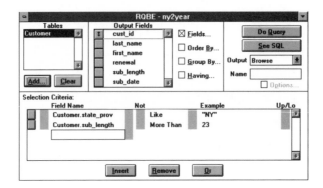

Add a new selection criterion

1 Click the blank box under Field Name.

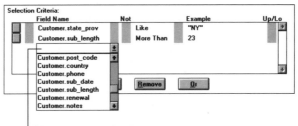

Click here to display the popup.

2 From the Field Name popup, select the Customer.sub_date field.

3 Press TAB twice to move to the comparison operator popup.

4 Click the down arrow next to the popup, and select More Than.

5 Press TAB once to move to the Example box.

6 Type **9/21/92**

The RQBE window looks like the following illustration.

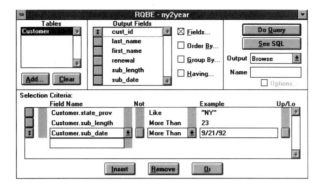

7 Click the Do Query push button to see the results of your query.

It appears that the promotion was not as successful as anticipated. Only one record matched the criteria you specified. But with a few more changes to this query, you can provide the Marketing department with some meaningful information about New York customers.

8 Double-click the Control-menu box in the Browse window.

Prioritizing Selection Criteria

There are now three selection criteria specified in this query: The state must be NY; it must be a two-year subscription or longer (more than 23 months); and the subscription date must be after 9/21/92. A record must satisfy all three criteria to be selected and displayed in the Browse window. If a record meets only one condition, it is not displayed in the Browse window.

By using the Or push button in the RQBE window, you can identify which conditions are optional and which conditions are required.

For example, the Marketing department wants to see the records for all New York customers who have either a subscription of more than 23 months or a subscription date after 9/21/92.

Specify optional selection criteria

1 In the RQBE window, click the Or push button.

The word "OR" appears at the bottom of the Field Name column.

2 Drag the Mover button for the word "OR" to immediately below the Customer.sub_length field.

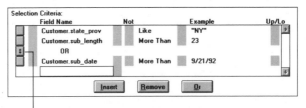

Drag the Mover button for OR here.

3   Click the blank box under Field Name.

4   From the Field Name popup, select the Customer.state_prov field.

5   Press TAB two times to move to the comparison operator popup.

The Like comparison operator is already selected. You do not need to change this field.

6   Press TAB again to move to the Example box.

7   Type **NY**

You need to repeat this criterion after the word "OR" to limit the search to only New York state customers with a subscription date after 9/21/92.

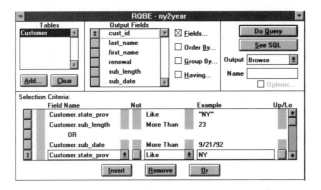

8   Click the Do Query push button to see the results of your query.

9   Double-click the Control-menu box in the Browse window.

Sorting by Multiple Fields

By sorting the selected records in a particular order, similar records appear together in the Browse window. For example, if a query sorts selected records by length of subscription, the records with the same subscription length are displayed together. To further organize each category of subscription, you can sort by an additional field. In this case, it might be useful to display the records within each subscription length by subscription date.

Sort by multiple fields

1 Click the Order By check box.

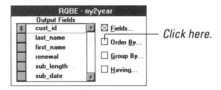

Click here.

The RQBE Order By dialog appears.

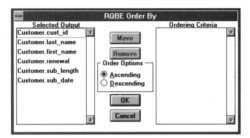

2 In the Selected Output list, select Customer.sub_length.

3 Click the Move push button.

Customer.sub_length is dimmed in the Selected Output list and appears in the Ordering Criteria list.

4 In the Selected Output list, select Customer.sub_date.

5 Click the Move push button.

Customer.sub_date is dimmed in the Selected Output list and appears in the Ordering Criteria list.

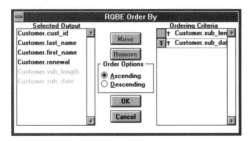

6 Click the OK push button to return to the RQBE window.

The numbers 1 and 2 next to the field names in the Output Fields list indicate that the records will be first ordered by Sub_length and then by Sub_date.

Sort fields

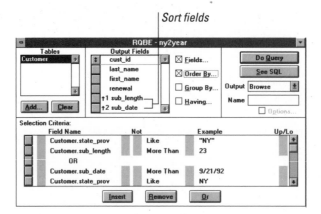

7 Click the Do Query push button to see the results of your query.

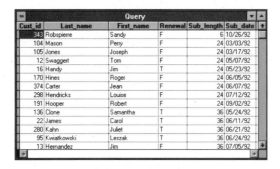

8 Double-click the Control-menu box in the Browse window.

Save the query file

1 Double-click the Control-menu box to close the RQBE window.

2 Click the Yes push button when you see the message about saving changes to NY2YEAR.QPR.

One Step Further

Queries are a great way to answer questions you get asked frequently. Use queries to answer these questions posed by Sweet Lil's Marketing department. Follow the general guidelines to get started.

Query 1: How many California customers have a one-year subscription?

1   Create a new query. In the RQBE window, specify selection criteria for which the Customer.sub_length field contains 12, and the Customer.state_prov field contains CA.

2   Do the query to see the number of selected records that appears in the status bar.

3   Save the query with the name **CA1YEAR.QPR**

Query 2: How many customers who do not live in California have a one-year subscription?

1   Modify the CA1YEAR.QPR query, by clicking the Not push button in the Selection Criteria area for the Customer.state_prov field.

2   Use the Save As option on the File menu to save the modified query with a new name. Call this query **NOTCA.QPR**

Query 3: How many New England customers have not renewed their subscriptions?

1   Create a new query. In the RQBE window, specify the following selection criteria:

Customer.state_prov contains **MA, ME, NH, CT, VT, RI**

Use the In comparison operator instead of the Like comparison operator. This operator selects records in which the Customer.state_prov field contains one of the state abbreviations listed in the Example box.

Customer.renewal contains **.F.** (False).

Tip   You could also click the Not push button operator and enter **.T.** (True) in the Example box for Customer.renewal.

---

2   Display these output fields:

State_prov

Sub_length

Cust_id

Last_name

3   Sort first by state and then by subscription length.

4   Save this query with the name **NESUBS.QPR**

If You Want to Continue to the Next Lesson

1   From the Window menu, choose Command.

2   In the Command window, type **close all**

3   Press ENTER.

The Close All command closes all windows and files which are open in all work areas.

4   Choose the Yes push button when you see the message asking whether you want to save your changes.

If You Want to Quit FoxPro for Windows for Now

▶   From the File menu, choose Exit.

Lesson Summary

To	Do this
Do a query	Use the Open option on the File menu to open the query file you want to use. From the RQBE window, click the Do Query push button.
Create a query	From the File menu, choose New. In the New dialog, click the Query radio button. Click the New push button.
Specify output fields	Open the RQBE window. Select the Fields dialog by clicking the Fields check box.
Remove output fields in a query one at a time	In the Selected Output list, select a field and click the Remove push button. *or* Double-click a field name in the Selected Output list.
Remove multiple fields	Click the first field you want to remove, and hold down the SHIFT key while you click the last field you want to remove. Click the Remove push button.
Remove multiple fields not listed together	Press the CTRL key while selecting each field you want to remove. Click the Remove push button.
Order output fields	Drag the Mover button for the field you want to move. Position the field in the list where you want it to appear.
Specify selection criteria	In the Selection Criteria area of the RQBE window, click the blank box under Field Name. Select the field you want. In the Example box, enter the contents of what the field should contain.

To	Do this
Save a query file	To save your query file when you close the RQBE window, click the Yes push button when you see the message about saving changes. In the Save Current Document As box, type the name for this query file. Click the Save push button to close the Save dialog and return to the CUSTOMER Browse window.
Specify optional selection criteria	In the RQBE window, click the Or push button. Drag the Mover button for the word "OR" to where you want it to appear in the sequence of selection criteria.
Sort by multiple field	Click the Order By check box. In the Selected Output list, select the field by which you want to sort. Click the Move push button. Click the OK push button to return to the RQBE window.

For more information on	See in *Microsoft FoxPro for Windows Getting Started*
Using the RQBE window	Chapter 2, Quick Start Chapter 5, Retrieving Your Data

For more information on	See in the *Microsoft FoxPro for Windows User's Guide*
Creating and using queries	Chapter 13, Querying Your Data with RQBE

Preview of the Next Lesson

In the next lesson, you will learn how to use queries to obtain on-screen and printed reports. You will learn how to create a basic report directly from the RQBE window. You will also learn how to use the Report Layout window to give your reports a polished, customized appearance by adding header and footer information, formatting and aligning text, and drawing lines and boxes.

Reporting Your Information

Up until now, you have concentrated on activities in which you view information on the screen. In this lesson, you will generate simple reports based on queries. Although you do not need to base a report on a query, this technique lets you compare the results of a query displayed in the Browse window with a query presented as a report.

In this lesson, you will use a report form to display the results of a query. After you specify whether you want fields arranged in rows or in columns, you will use formatting and alignment techniques to emphasize parts of the report, and use lines and boxes to create additional visual interest. If you have a printer connected to your computer, you will also learn how to print your report.

You will learn how to:

- Use a query to generate a report.
- Create a report form.
- Arrange fields in a report form.
- Format text in a report form.
- Add a box in a report form.
- View the report in the Page Preview window.
- Change the report output destination.

Estimated lesson time: 45 minutes

If you closed FoxPro for Windows at the end of the last lesson

▶ Start FoxPro for Windows by double-clicking the FoxPro for Windows icon.

Open the CUSTOMER table

1 From the Window menu, choose View.

2 In the View window, click the Open push button.

3 In the Directory list, double-click PRACTICE to make it the current directory.

   PRACTICE is already the current directory if you did not exit FoxPro for Windows at the end of the last lesson.

4 In the Select A Table list, select the table called CUSTOMER.DBF.

5 Click the Open push button.

Using a Query to Generate a Report

So far, you have provided information to your peers in the Marketing department at Sweet Lil's by simply retrieving the desired information and displaying it in the Browse window on the screen. Now, the vice president of Marketing requires information from your tables for an important meeting with senior management. Just retrieving records on the screen will not do; you need to provide professional-looking reports that are easy to read.

A report is more highly formatted than query results, and it is usually intended to be printed. Creating a report from a query involves using the RQBE window to direct the query results to a *report/label* rather than the Browse window.

Create a simple report based on a query file that is similar to the one you created in the previous lesson.

Open an existing query

1   From the File menu, choose Open.

2   In the List Files Of Type popup, select Query.

3   In the File Name list, select LSNQ04.QPR.

4   Click the Open push button.

    The RQBE window appears.

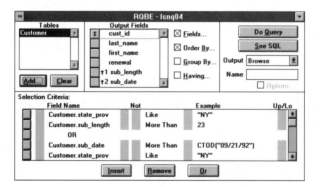

Save the query with a new name

Before you make any changes to this query, save it with a new name. By working in a copy, you keep the original file intact, so you can repeat this lesson if you wish.

1   From the File menu, choose Save As.

    The Save As dialog appears.

2   In the Save Current Document As box, type **SWEETQ04.QPR**

3   Click the Save push button.

Direct output to a report/label

▶ In the Output popup, select Report/Label.

Click here to select Report/Label.

Clear the window

To get a better view of the report in the next step, clear the FoxPro for Windows logo from the desktop.

▶ From the Window menu, choose Clear.

Generate the report

▶ Click the Do Query push button.

FoxPro for Windows displays the selected records in a report format in the application window. Depending on the kind of display you are using, you might need to press any key to see additional records in the report.

Return to the RQBE window

▶ After you scroll to the last record in the report, the RQBE window appears. To return to the RQBE window right away, press ESC.

View the report

1 Minimize the RQBE window.

2 Click the View window to make it active.

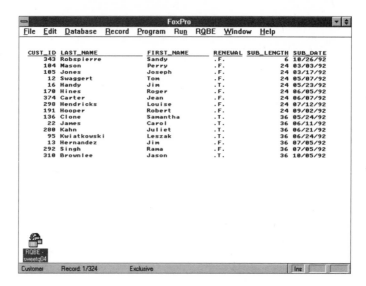

3   From the Window menu, choose Hide so you can see your report.

4   Double-click the RQBE icon to restore the RQBE window.

Creating a Report Form

A *report form* allows you to specify the arrangement of fields either in rows or in columns. You can specify header and footer information to appear on each page of the printed report. Report forms also have the added benefit of allowing you to format text and create design elements, such as lines and boxes, to emphasize information.

Create a new report form based on a query

1   In the RQBE window, be sure Output is set to Report/Label.

2   Click the Options check box.

Click here.

The RQBE Display Options dialog appears.

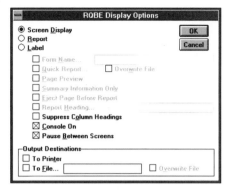

In this dialog, you can choose where you want the report displayed: on the screen, as a report (to be printed), or as labels (to be printed).

3   Click the Report radio button.

When you choose Report, additional check box options become available.

4   Click the Quick Report check box.

The RQBE Quick Report dialog appears.

Displays fields in columns,
as in the Browse window.

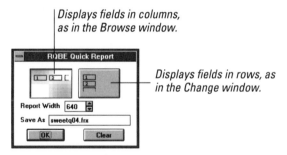

Displays fields in rows, as
in the Change window.

5   Click the large push button on the left to display records in a format of rows and columns.

6   Click the OK push button to return to the RQBE Display Options dialog.

The Form Name box now contains the name of the form, PRACTICE\SWEETQ04.FRX. However, you need to do the query before the report form is actually created. And the form must be created before you can open and modify it.

7   Click the OK push button to return to the RQBE window.

8   Click the Do Query push button.

The report appears in the Page Preview window.

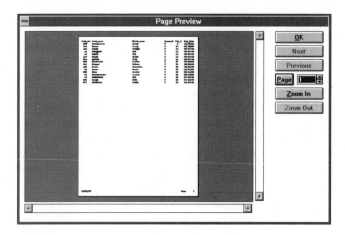

Using the Page Preview Window

In the RQBE Display Options dialog, the Page Preview check box was already selected. This means that your report displays on the screen as it would appear when printed on a printer.

Get a close-up view of the page

The pointer looks like a magnifying glass when you position it inside the display area.

You can also choose the Zoom In push button.

▶ Click anywhere in the display area to get a close-up view of the report.

If you click the text area of the page, you see that part of the page close up.

See the entire page

You can also choose the Zoom Out push button.

▶ Click anywhere in the display area to see the entire page again.

Return to the RQBE window

1   Click the OK push button to return to the RQBE window.

2   From the File menu, choose Save.

3   Minimize the RQBE window, so you can return to it later.

Changing the Report Layout

There are a number of features you can add to the report form to improve its appearance. For example, by adding headers, you can include information about the report that will be printed at the top of every page. With footers, you can include information that is printed at the bottom of every page.

Open the report form you created earlier in this lesson, and change header information in the Report Layout window.

Open the new report form

1   From the File menu, choose Open.

2   In the List Files Of Type popup, select Report.

3   In the File Name list, select SWEETQ04.FRX.

Be sure PRACTICE is the current directory.

4   Click the Open push button.

The Report Layout window for SWEETQ04.FRX appears.

Using the Report Layout Window

You use the Report Layout window to customize the appearance of a report form. The Report Layout window contains a toolbox that allows you to create, edit, and manipulate objects that appear in the window.

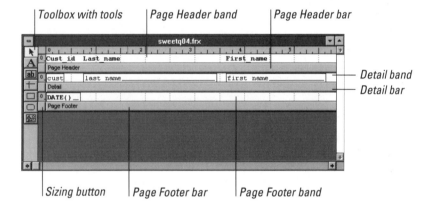

Modifying the Header

In the Report Layout window, header information appears above the Page Header bar. FoxPro for Windows automatically displays the output field names in the Page Header band.

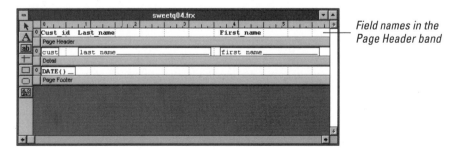

Change the header to contain the name of the report, the current date, and column titles instead of field names.

Delete existing header information

1   Click the title for the first field, Cust_id.

The field title is an *object*. An object is selected when you click it and handles appear around it.

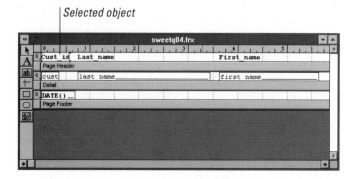

Selected object

2   SHIFT-CLICK each column title in the Page Header band until all the titles are selected.

3   Press DELETE to remove these objects.

4   Scroll to the left so that the Report Layout window looks like the following illustration.

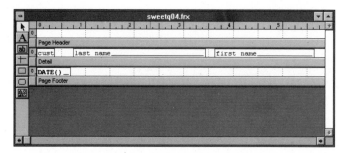

Changing the Height of the Page Header Band

Before you rearrange the objects in the Page Header band, you need to increase the size of the band so that you can see the grid lines and move fields.

Increase the header size

▶   Drag the Sizing button for the Page Header band down about one inch.

— *Drag from here.*

— *Drag to here.*

Entering Text in the Report Layout Window

You use the text tool to enter text in the window. When you click the text tool in the toolbox, the pointer changes to an I-beam. Position the pointer where you want the text to appear, and click to place the insertion point. Then start typing.

Do not worry about making an exact placement of the text. Once you enter the text, what you type becomes an object that you can move.

Enter new text

Text tool

1   Click the text tool.

2   Click an insertion point about two squares in from the left and one square down from the top.

Note   If you cannot see lines displaying a grid in the Report Layout window, choose Ruler/Grid from the Report menu. In the Ruler/Grid dialog, click the Yes push button under Ruler Lines. Click the OK push button to close the dialog and return to the Report Layout window.

---

3   Type **New York Results**

Position text

Pointer tool

1   Click the pointer tool.

2   Select the text object you have just entered.

3   Drag it to the top of the window at the 2-inch mark.

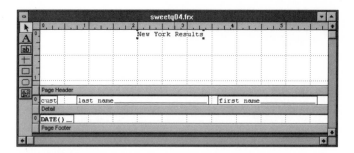

Position a field

▶ Drag the DATE() field in the Page Footer band to the Page Header band. Position it at the top right edge.

Enter new column headings

Default column headings are the same as the field names. Because these names are rather cryptic to someone who is not familiar with your table and the contents of the fields, you want more descriptive column headings for your report.

After you complete entering new column headings, your Report Layout window will look like the following illustration.

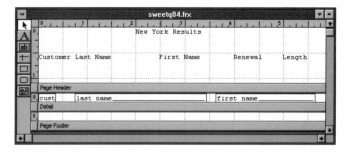

Text tool

1 Double-click the text tool.

Tip   By double-clicking the text tool, the tool stays active until you select another tool or use the scroll arrows to scroll the window. Use this technique so that you do not have to click the tool after every object when creating several text objects at once.

---

2 Click the pointer at the left margin one square down from the top, just below the dotted line.

3 Type **Customer**

4 Click the pointer one and a half squares from the left and one square down from the top.

5 Type **Last Name**

6 Click the pointer five squares from the left and one square down from the top.

7 Type **First Name**

8 Click the pointer eight squares from the left and one square down from the top.

9 Type **Renewal**

10 Click the pointer ten squares from the left and one square down from the top.

11 Type **Length**

12 Click the pointer twelve squares from the left and one square down from the top.

13 Type **Subscription Date**

The Report Layout window looks like the following illustration.

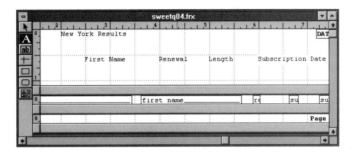

Preview the report

1 From the Report menu, choose Page Preview.

A preview of the printed report looks like the following illustration.

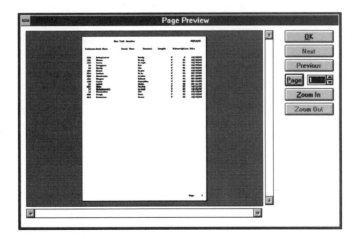

2   Click the OK push button to return to the Report Layout window.

Adjusting Column Width

When you examine the report in the Preview window, you may notice that the columns of data do not line up well under the column titles. This is because the width of each column is set to whatever field length was specified in the table. By adjusting the column width of each field in the Detail band of the Report Layout window and by repositioning the fields, you can line up each column of data under the column heading you laid out in the Page Header band.

Tip   The first time you click in the Report Layout window, the window becomes active. You need to click again to select an object or a tool.

Adjust field column width

1   Click the selection pointer in the toolbox, and then select the Cust_id object in the Detail band.

2   Drag the object to the right until the field is centered under the Customer column heading.

3   Select the Last_name object in the Detail band.

4   Drag the handle on the right to the left until the field fits within three squares.

5   Select the First_name object in the Detail band.

6   Drag the object to the left until the field fits under the First_name column heading, and adjust the width so that it is two squares wide.

7   Select the Renewal object in the Detail band.

8   Drag the object so that it is under the Renewal column heading, and adjust the column width so that it is one square wide.

9   Select the Sub_length object in the Detail band.

10   Drag the object to the left until the field is centered under the Length column heading.

11   Select the Sub_date object in the Detail band.

12   Drag the object to the left until the field fits under the Subscription Date column heading.

Preview the report

1   From the Report menu, choose Page Preview.

A preview of the printed report looks like the following illustration.

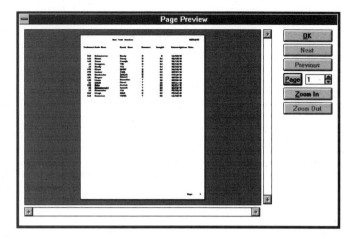

2   Click the OK push button to return to the Report Layout window.

Formatting Text in a Report Form

To improve the appearance of the report, you can change the size, alignment, and the font of text in the report. These changes do more than make the report more attractive. Such enhancements make the report easier to read, and, in many cases, the information you are attempting to convey comes across clearer.

Format the report title

Establish a context for this report in the mind of your audience by drawing attention to the title of the report.

1   Click the report title, "New York Results," to select it.

2   From the Object menu, choose Font.

The Font dialog appears.

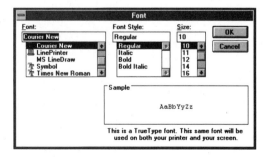

3 In the Font Style popup, select Bold.

4 In the Size popup, select 12.

5 Click the OK push button.

Format column headings

Distinguish the column titles from the data by making the column headings in the header bold. You can select all the column titles at once by using the selection *marquee*. A marquee is the dotted box that appears when you drag a rectangle around a group of objects to select them.

You can also SHIFT-CLICK each column title to select all of these objects.

1 Drag the selection marquee starting from below and to the right of the Subscription Date column heading in the Page Header band to above and to the left of the Customer column heading.

All the column headings are selected.

2 From the Object menu, choose Font.

3 In the Font Style popup, select Bold.

4 Click the OK push button.

Format report detail

Add visual interest by aligning the data in a column.

1 Click the Renewal field in the Detail band.

2 From the Object menu, choose Text Alignment.

3 In the Text Alignment cascading menu, choose Center.

A check mark appears in front of "Center" indicating it is selected. This means the data in this column will appear centered when you print this report.

Preview the report

1 From the Report menu, choose Page Preview.

A preview of the printed report looks like the following illustration.

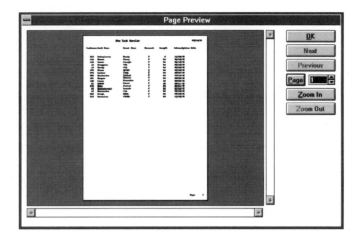

2   Click the OK push button to return to the Report Layout window.

Adding Graphics in a Report Form

Another way to add visual interest to a report is to use graphic elements, such as lines and boxes.

Add a line to the report

Draw a line under the column headings in the Page Header band.

Line tool

1   Click the line tool in the toolbox.

2   Drag the pointer beginning at the Customer column heading to the end of the Subscription Date column heading.

When you release the mouse button, the line appears.

3   Scroll to the left so that the Report Layout window looks like the following illustration.

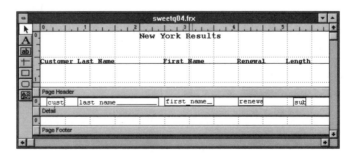

Position the line

▶ With the line selected, drag the line downward to the ¾-inch mark.

Change the line width

1 With the line still selected, from the Object menu, choose Pen.

2 From the Pen cascading menu, choose 4 Point.

Add a box to the report

Box tool

1 Click the box tool in the toolbox.

2 Drag a box to surround the report title.

Placing Objects in the Report Layout Window

As you drew the box, you may have noticed that the box was almost "forced" to be a certain size. Similarly, when you placed text, the object seemed to "snap" in place. By default, the Report Layout window positions objects on the grid at regular intervals. To give you complete flexibility over placing objects, you can turn off the Snap To Grid option.

Turn off Snap To Grid

▶ From the Report menu, choose Snap To Grid.

Making this selection removes the check mark in front of this command on the menu.

Tip   To make fine adjustments one pixel at a time without turning off the Snap To Grid setting, you can use the arrow keys on your keyboard to position an object.

Send box to the back

The last object you created, the box, is actually in front of the report title text. You can see the text "through" the box object because the box is transparent. To work with the report title text that is currently behind the box, you need to send the box object to the back so that the text object comes to the front.

▶ With the box selected, from the Object menu, choose Send To Back.

Position the text

The report title text is not centered vertically in the box. Move the text closer to the bottom of the box.

1 Select the report title text.

2 Drag the text until it is positioned near the bottom edge of the box.

Adjust box size

With the Snap To Grid selection off, you can make fine adjustments to the size and placement of objects in the Report Layout window. Adjust the size of the box so that it is wider around the report title text.

1 Select the box.

2 Drag the right handle to the 4-inch mark.

3 Drag the left handle to the 1½-inch mark.

The Report Layout window looks like the following illustration.

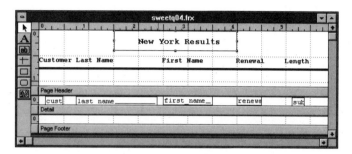

4 From the Report menu, choose Page Preview.

A preview of the printed report looks like the following illustration.

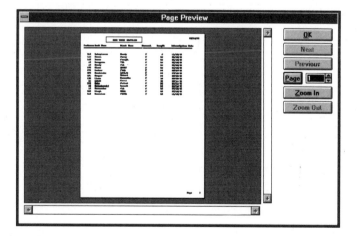

5 Click the OK push button to return to the Report Layout window.

Close the Report Layout window and save your report

1   Double-click the Control-menu box to close the Report Layout window.

2   Click the Yes push button when FoxPro for Windows asks whether you want to save changes to this report form.

Changing the Output Destination

Up to this point, you have been directing the report to go to the Page Preview screen whenever you press the Do Query push button in the RQBE window. To have the report go to the printer connected to your computer, you need to change the output destination.

Send the report to a printer

If you do not have a printer connected to your computer, skip this procedure.

1   Double-click the RQBE icon to restore the RQBE window.

2   In the RQBE window, click the Options check box.

3   In the RQBE Display Options dialog, clear the Page Preview check box.

The Output Destination options at the bottom of the dialog become enabled.

4   Click the To Printer check box.

5   Click the OK push button.

6   In the RQBE window, click the Do Query push button to have the report printed on your printer.

The Print dialog appears.

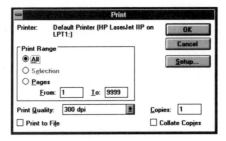

7   In the Print dialog, click the OK push button.

8   Double-click the Control-menu box to close the RQBE window.

9   Click the Yes push button when you see the message asking whether you want to save changes to this query.

One Step Further

The vice president of Marketing at Sweet Lil's is impressed with the report you created. Now she wants to see a report based on another query, called OSFQ04.QPR.

1   Open the RQBE window for this query. Before you make any changes, save the query with the new name **Q04NESUB.QPR**

Hint: Use the Save As command from the File menu.

2   Direct the output to go to Report/Label.

3   Click the Options check box to display the RQBE Display Options dialog.

4   Click the Report radio button.

5   If you have a printer connected to your computer, select To Printer for the output destination.

6   Choose Quick Report and specify a single-column format for the report (the large right push button).

7   Do the query to create the report form.

8   From the File menu, choose Open, select Report from the List Files Of Type popup, and then select Q04NESUB.FRX from the popup list.

9   In the Report Layout window make the following changes to the report form:

Report title: New England Renewals (Bold, 12 point)

Row headings: State, Length, Customer ID, Name (Italics)

10   Drag the Footer bar down to add a ½-inch space.

11   With the line tool, create a line between each detail record.

12   With the text tool, type the name of the query file in the footer.

If You Want to Continue to the Next Lesson

1   From the Window menu, choose Command.

2   In the Command window, type **close all**

3   Press ENTER.

The Close All command closes all windows and files which are open in all work areas.

4   Click the Yes push button when you see the message asking whether you want to save your changes.

If You Want to Quit FoxPro for Windows for Now

1   From the File menu, choose Exit.

2   Click the Yes push button when you see the message asking whether you want to save your changes.

Lesson Summary

To	Do this
Create a report based on a query	Open an existing query, and then select Report/Label in the Output popup. Click the Options check box. In the RQBE Display Options dialog, click the Report radio button. Click the Quick Report check box to select the arrangement of fields. Specify the name of the report form you want to create. Click the OK push button until you return to the RQBE window. Click the Do Query push button.
Get a close-up view of the page in Page Preview	Click anywhere in the display area to get a close-up view of the report. *or* Choose the Zoom In push button.
See the entire page	Click anywhere in the display area to see the report. *or* Choose the Zoom Out push button.
See other pages	Click in the Page box, and use the spinner control to display the number of the page you want.
Create a new report	From the File menu, choose New. In the New dialog, click the Report radio button. Click the New push button to display the Report Layout window.
Change the report layout for an existing query	From the File menu, choose Open. In the List Files Of Type popup, select Report. Double-click a report from the File Name list to display the Report Layout window.
Enter text in the Report Layout window	Click the text tool in the toolbox. Position the I-beam where you want the text to appear, and click to place an insertion point. Then start typing.
Position an object	Click an object to select it, and then drag it to the new location.
Adjust column width	Select the field object for the column in the Detail band. Drag the handle until the field is the size you want.

To	Do this
Format text in a report	Select a text object. From the Object menu, choose Font. In the Font dialog, make your selections to change the style, font, and size of the text.
Add a line to the report	Click the line tool in the toolbox. Drag the pointer to create the line. Drawing a line in the Detail area causes the line to be repeated for each record in the report.
Add a box to the report	Click the box tool in the toolbox. Drag the pointer to create the box.
Turn off Snap To Grid	From the Report menu, choose Snap To Grid.
Send an object to the back	With an object selected, choose Send To Back from the Object menu.
Send the report to a printer	In the RQBE window, click the Options check box. In the RQBE Display Options dialog, clear the Page Preview check box. Click the To Printer check box. Click the OK push button to return to the RQBE window. Click the Do Query button to have the report printed on your printer.

For more information on	See in *Microsoft FoxPro for Windows Getting Started*
Reporting with RQBE	Chapter 2, Quick Start Chapter 6, Reporting on Your Data

For more information on	See in the *Microsoft FoxPro for Windows User's Guide*
Reports	Chapter 4, Database Menu (Report) Chapter 14, Designing Reports and Labels

Preview of the Next Lesson

The lessons in Part 2 of this book help you gain more control over using and reporting information in your tables. You will learn how to create your own table and change the structure of the table by adding and deleting fields. You will combine and obtain information located in multiple tables. In addition, you will learn new ways to add features to your reports that improve their appearance as well as the quality of information they provide.

Review & Practice

The lessons in this part of the book introduced you to the basics of working with tables. The Review & Practice lesson that follows will help you prepare for the lessons in the next part of the book. This is a less structured scenario in which you can practice and refine your skills. Follow the general guidelines—the rest is up to you.

Part 1 Review & Practice

Before you begin working in a table of your own, practice the skills you learned in Part 1 by working through the basics of using tables. You will start by opening a table and moving around in the Browse window. Then you will locate and modify specific information stored in fields and records, and add and delete records. You will also use a query to retrieve the information you need, and then create a report form to display records the way you want.

Scenario

The Review & Practice sections of this book are based on a realistic scenario for which you can use FoxPro to provide database information. As the PC Support manager at Sweet Lil's, you will help the Human Resources staff manage their information. In this Review & Practice section, you work with a table that contains Sweet Lil's employee information. Follow the general guidelines provided in each step. If you need help, use the table at the end of each step for references to additional information in the lessons.

You will review and practice how to:

- Open a table.
- Use the Browse window.
- Add and delete records.
- Locate records.
- Display records based on a query you create.
- Direct query results to a report form you create using Quick Report.

Estimated lesson time: 45 minutes

Step 1:   Display Database Information

The Human Resources staff has employee information stored in a table. Use the View window to open and browse through the table to become familiar with the information.

Open a table

▶ Use the View window to open a table called EMPLOYEE.DBF. This file is located in the REVIEW directory under PRACTICE. In the Open dialog, double-click REVIEW in the Directory list to display the list of tables.

Browse through a table

▶ Use the Browse window to view your table.

Adjust the size of the Browse window

▶ Drag the lower-right corner of the window to the right so that you can see at least 12 records and the Job_title field.

For more information on	See
Opening a Table	Lesson 1
Browsing a Table	Lesson 1
Modifying the Browse Window	Lesson 1

Step 2:   Modify Table Information

Update the table to include the following changes:

▶ Marina Ortiz just got married. Change her last name to "Carvelle."

▶ Bill Johnson, employee ID 18, has improved his performance in the 4th quarter. Open the Comment field for this employee, and add the following:
Increased personal sales by 36%, 4th quarter, 1992.

▶ Last year's President's Productivity Award went to Carolyn Smith. This year, the award goes to Chris Anderson, the executive assistant. Open the Comment field for Carolyn Smith, and use copy and paste techniques to enter an award message in the Comment field for this year's winner. Be sure to change the year to "1993."

▶ Here is the top part of a form for a new employee hired in Shipping. Enter the following information for the employee.

```
┌─────────────────────────────────────────────────────────┐
│            Sweet Lil's Employee Personnel Summary         │
│                                                           │
│   First Name:  Sandra                                     │
│   Last Name:   Carpenter                                  │
│   Department:  Shipping (SHIP)   Employee #:  29          │
│   Salary:      2800              Hire Date:   02/02/93    │
│   Job Title:   Shipping Coordinator                       │
│                                                           │
└─────────────────────────────────────────────────────────┘
```

For more information on	See
Making Entries in a Field	Lesson 1
Working with Memo Fields	Lesson 1
Adding New Records	Lesson 2

Step 3: Delete Records

Two people have left Sweet Lil's and should be removed from the EMPLOYEE table. Use the Locate option and your knowledge of the Expression Builder dialog to find individual records in the table.

Locate a record with the Expression Builder dialog

Lisa Martinez, the vice president of Operations, has left the company. Use the Locate option on the Record menu, and specify search criteria in the Expression Builder dialog. You can search for "Martinez" in the Last Name field.

Use these guidelines to locate and delete records:

1 Mark the record for Ms. Martinez for deletion.

2 On the Record menu, use the Goto option to jump to record 26. Mark this record for deletion as well.

3 You just learned that Ben McIntyre is not leaving, but James Horton is. Unmark record 26, and mark record 25, instead.

4 To permanently remove the marked records from the table, use the Pack option on the Database menu.

Change the contents of a field in many records

▶ As a result of a recent reorganization, the Shipping and Operations departments have merged. Use the Replace option on the Record menu to change all occurrences of "SHIP" in the Department field to "OPER".

For more information on	See
Locating a Record	Lesson 2
Jumping to a Record	Lesson 2
Deleting Records	Lesson 2
Changing Your Mind	Lesson 2
One Step Further (Using Replace)	Lesson 2

Step 4: Retrieve Your Information

The Human Resources staff wants to know which employees earn the highest salaries in each department, except for the Executive department. Create a query that displays these records.

Create a query

1   On the File menu, use the New option to create a new file. Then specify that you want to create a query, so the RQBE window appears.

2   Remove the First Name and Last Name fields from the Output Fields list, so that employee names are not displayed in the window when you do the query (you want to keep salary information confidential). Return to the RQBE window.

Hint   Click the Fields check box to display the RQBE Select Fields dialog.

---

3   In the Output Fields list, use the Mover button to drag the fields so that the columns appear in this order:

Department
Salary
Hire_date
Empl_id
Job_title
Comments

Order by multiple fields

▶   Order the fields so that the records are first ordered by department name (Department field) in ascending order. So that the highest salaries in each department appear first in each group of records, select the Salary field in descending order. Return to the RQBE window when you are done.

Hint   Click the Order By check box to display the RQBE Order By dialog.

Specify selection conditions

▶ Because you want to see records for all departments *except* the Executive depart-ment, use the Not comparison operator after you specify the Department field in the Selection Criteria area of the window. Enter "EXEC" in the Example column to exclude records for the Executive staff.

Do the query and close the Browse window

▶ Choose the Do Query button. After your records display, close the Browse window.

Save a query

1   From the File menu, choose Save. In the Directory dialog, be sure REVIEW is the current directory.

2   Save your query with the name **REV01.QPR**

Prioritize selection conditions

You realize that you only wanted to exclude the executive salaries, not the executive support personnel, who earn significantly less than the executives.

▶ Add selection criteria to include these records in the query. Because executive sup-port personnel earn less than $3000 per month, you can specify selection criteria to include records from the Executive department only if the salary is under $3000.

Hint   In the blank field in the Field Name column, click the Or push button. Specify that the Department field should contain "EXEC." In the next blank line, specify that the Salary field should contain a value less than 3000.

Do the query and close the Browse window

▶ Choose the Do Query button. After your records are displayed, close the Browse window. Then save your query.

For more information on	See
Retrieving Data with Queries	Lesson 3
Creating Your Own Query	Lesson 3
Understanding the RQBE Window	Lesson 3
Removing Fields from a Query	Lesson 3
Ordering Output Fields	Lesson 3
Specifying Selection Criteria	Lesson 3

For more information on	See
Saving a Query	Lesson 3
Prioritizing Selection Criteria	Lesson 3

Step 5: Report Your Information

This is exactly the information the Human Resources manager needs to provide for an upcoming salary review meeting. Make a report based on this query.

Use a query to generate a report

▶ With the RQBE window for your query still open, select Report/Label from the Output popup.

Create a report form

1   An easy way to generate a simple report from a query is to use Quick Report. Click the Options check box to see the RQBE Display Options dialog. Choose the Report radio button, and then click the Quick Report check box. In the RQBE Quick Report dialog, click the large button on the left to display records in a format of rows and columns.

2   Choose the Do Query button to display the report in the Page Preview window.

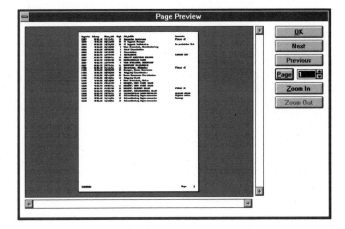

Get a close-up view of the report

▶ Click anywhere in the screen to get a close-up view of the report.

For more information on	See
Using a Query to Generate a Report	Lesson 4
Creating a Report Form	Lesson 4
Using the Page Preview Window	Lesson 4

Step 6: Modify the Report Form

Customize the appearance of the report by changing the report form you created with Quick Report.

Open the report form

▶ From the File menu, choose Open. After you verify that the REVIEW directory is open, select Report from the List Files Of Type popup. Then double-click the report file called REV01.FRX.

Change header information

1 Select all the objects in the Page Header band. Press the DEL key to remove these objects.

2 Use the text tool to create a report title centered near the top of the Report Layout window. For the report title, type **Department Salaries.** Position the text near the top of the Report Layout window, and center it.

3 Drag the Sizing button for the Header bar downward about one inch.

4 Drag the DATE() field in the Page Footer band to the Page Header band. Position it at the upper-right edge.

Text tool

Enter new column headings

▶ Use the text tool to type the following column titles:

Use this heading	Above this field
Date Hired	Hire_date
ID	Empl_id
Title	Job_title

Enter new text in the Page Footer band

Use the text tool to type the company name in the Page Footer band. For the footer, type **Sweet Lil's, Inc.** With the pointer tool, position the text as needed so that it appears in approximately the same location where the DATE() field was located.

Improve the appearance of the report

Make the following changes to the report so that it is easier to read:

▶ Drag the right handle of the Department field so that the column is as wide as the column heading.

▶ Make the title of the report stand out more clearly by formatting the text bold and by using 14 as the point size.

▶ Make the column titles stand out more clearly by formatting the text bold and by using 12 as the point size.

▶ Use the line tool to draw a line just below the column titles.

▶ Use the box tool to create a box around the report title. So that the report title text appears neatly inside the box, follow these guidelines:

 ▪ Turn off Snap To Grid.

 ▪ Select the box object, and send it to the back of the report title.

 ▪ Position the text and size the box as necessary.

Preview the Report Layout

▶ From the Report menu, choose Page Preview.

Close the Report Layout window and save your report

▶ Double-click the Control-menu box, and answer Yes when you are prompted to save your changes to the report.

Close the RQBE window and save your query

▶ Double-click the Control-menu box, and answer Yes when you are prompted to save your changes to the query.

For more information on	See
Changing the Report Layout	Lesson 4
Using the Report Layout Window	Lesson 4
Entering Text in the Report Layout Window	Lesson 4
Adjusting Column Width	Lesson 4
Formatting Text in a Report Form	Lesson 4

For more information on	See
Adding Graphics in a Report Form	Lesson 4
Placing Objects in the Report Layout Window	Lesson 4

If You Want to Continue to the Next Lesson

1   From the Window menu, choose Command.

2   In the Command window, type **close all**

3   Press ENTER.

The Close All command closes all windows and files which are open in all work areas.

4   Click the Yes button when you see the message asking whether you want to save your changes.

If You Want to Quit FoxPro for Now

▶   From the File menu, choose Exit.

Part

2 Organizing Database Information

Creating Your Own Table

In previous lessons, you worked with tables that were created for you and were provided on the exercise disk that comes with this book. But unless you want to maintain the same information as Sweet Lil's, these files are not very helpful to you. You need to know how to make your own table files.

In this lesson, you will establish a table structure for a table of your own. You will learn about different types of fields and the information they can contain. After you enter some information in your table, you will learn how to change the structure of the table by changing field lengths, and adding and deleting fields.

You will learn how to:

- Define a table structure.
- Specify different field types.
- Modify the table structure.
- Change a field length.
- Add a new field.
- Delete a field.
- Rearrange fields.

Estimated lesson time: 35 minutes

If you closed FoxPro for Windows at the end of the last lesson

▶ Start FoxPro for Windows by double-clicking the FoxPro for Windows icon.

Defining a New Table Structure

Creating your own table structure means deciding what kinds of information you want to include in the table. For example, do you want your table to contain names, addresses, amounts, dates, and comments? Do you (or others) want to use the table to keep track of products on hand and products purchased? The possibilities of what you can enter and store in a table are endless. Next, you need to determine how much information (in terms of characters) you will require for a given field and what the name of each field should be.

Sweet Lil's has been growing rapidly as new products are developed practically every day. The director of Manufacturing had been keeping bonbon information on 3" x 5" index cards, but this system is getting a little unwieldy. As a result, the director of

Manufacturing has decided to use FoxPro for Windows to keep track of the different kinds of bonbons made at Sweet Lil's. As the PC Support Manager, you have been asked to create the table for Manufacturing.

Create a new table

1   From the File menu, choose New.

2   In the New dialog, be sure that Table/DBF is selected.

3   Click the New push button.

The Table Structure dialog appears.

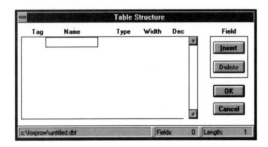

Specifying Fields

Creating a table structure sounds complicated, but it is no more difficult than deciding the names of the fields, the type of data the fields will contain, and the size the fields need to be. You can create fields that can contain specific kinds of information. These field types fall into the following categories.

Field type	Description	Examples
Character	Use this type when the information is not going to be used in a calculation or the information is not a date. (Any type of alphanumeric data is valid.) This is the default field type.	Product names; names; addresses; numbers with the same number of digits that are not to be used in calculations, such as ZIP Codes, phone numbers, and Social Security numbers.
Numeric	Use this type when the field will contain numbers you might use in a calculation (as in a total or an average). You can specify the number of decimal places.	Quantity, amount, cost, rate, interest.

Field type	Description	Examples
Float	Use this type for scientific or engineering data used in calculations that must be accurate beyond 16 significant digits (but otherwise this type is the same as the numeric field type).	Coefficient of expansion, atomic weight.
Date	Use this type when the field will contain a date.	Start date, expiration date, birth date.
Logical	Use this type when the field will contain either a true or a false (yes or no) value.	Renewal? (T/F), Retired? (Y/N)
Memo	Use this type when you want to enter comments that can be of almost unlimited length. Unlike the other field types, memo fields cannot be sorted.	Description, notes, comments.

The default field length is displayed when you first enter a new field name. You can change the size of a character field to accommodate up to 255 characters.

When defining fields for a new table, the best place to look for field specifications is on any form you might already be using to collect or store information. In this case, the bonbon index cards provide the field details you need to define the table structure.

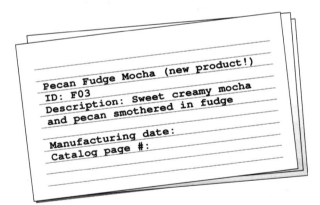

Enter a field name

You do not have to be especially creative when determining field names. Because you are limited to 10 characters, keep the names succinct, but unique from one another.

1   In the Name column, type **bonbon_id**

A field name can contain letters and numbers, but it *must* begin with a letter. Except for the underline (_), it cannot contain spaces or punctuation.

As you type your entry, default settings for the type of field (Type) and size of field (Width) are displayed in the popups.

2   Press TAB to move to the Type popup.

Remember, if you change your mind about a field name, its length, or its type, you can change the structure of the table later (even after it contains data).

Specify a field type

In the Type popup, you can select the field type that identifies the kind of data this field will contain.

1   Click the down arrow next to the Type popup to display the list of field types from which you can choose.

The correct field type for this field, Character, is already selected.

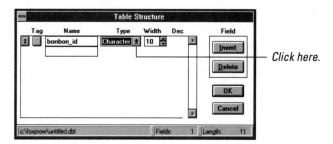

Click here.

2   Click the down arrow to close the Type popup.

3   Press TAB to move to the Width column.

Specify the field length

Use the spinner control to specify the maximum length of this field. This field will contain a three-character ID.

You can also type a value in the field, without using the spinner control.

▶   Click the down arrow of the spinner control until "3" appears in the field.

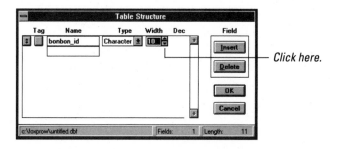

Click here.

You have finished entering the specifications for the first field in your new table. The Table Structure dialog looks like the following illustration.

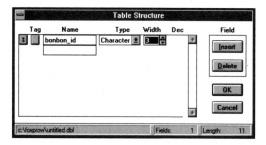

Specify another field

Enter a field to identify the name of this bonbon.

1 Press TAB to insert another field in the table structure.

2 In the Name column, type **bon_name**

3 Press TAB to move to the Type column.

The correct field type for this field, Character, is already selected.

4 Press TAB to move to the Width column.

5 Click the up arrow of the spinner control until "15" appears in the field.

Specify another field

Enter a field to identify the page in the current catalog where this bonbon is first described.

1 Press TAB to insert another field.

2 In the Name column, type **page_num**

3 Press TAB to move to the Type column.

The correct field type for this field, Character, is already selected.

Even though it might seem that a page number would belong in a number field, it is not a value that you would use in a calculation. For example, you would not expect to add up all the page numbers and get a total that means anything. Nor would you subtract one page number from another. For all intents and purposes, this entry is best described as a character field.

4 Press TAB to move to the Width column.

5 Click the down arrow of the spinner control until "2" appears in the field.

Specify a date field

Enter a field to identify when this bonbon was first manufactured.

1   Press TAB to insert another field in the table structure.

2   In the Name column, type **mfg_date**

3   Press TAB to move to the Type column.

4   Select "Date" from the popup.

Date fields have a field length of eight that you cannot change.

Specify a numeric field

Enter a field to identify the cost to produce an individual bonbon.

1   Press TAB to insert another field.

2   In the Name column, type **cost**

3   Press TAB to move to the Type column.

You can save time by entering the first character of the field type you want, rather than scrolling to the selection. This action also automatically moves you to the next column.

4   Select "Numeric" from the popup.

5   Press TAB to move to the Width column.

6   Click the down arrow of the spinner control until "4" appears in the field.

7   Press TAB to move to the Dec column.

In the Dec column, you can specify the number of decimal places you want to allow for this field.

8   Click the up arrow of the spinner control until "2" appears in the field.

Specify another numeric field

Enter a field to identify the number of calories in an individual bonbon.

1   Press TAB to insert another field.

2   In the Name column, type **calories**

3   Press TAB to move to the Type column.

4   Select Numeric from the popup.

5   Press TAB to move to the Width column.

6   Click the down arrow of the spinner control until "4" appears in the field.

7   Press TAB to skip over the Dec column.

Specify a memo field

Enter a field to contain a catalog-style description of an individual bonbon.

1   Press TAB to insert another field.

2   In the Name column, type **descript**

3 Press TAB to move to the Type column.

4 Select "Memo" from the popup.

Even though memo fields have a fixed field length of 10 characters (as defined in the Table Structure dialog), a memo field itself can have many pages of text stored in it.

Save your table

After entering all the field types and specifications for your new table, close the Table Structure dialog, and save the table.

1 Click the OK push button.

The Save As dialog appears.

2 In the Directory list, double-click PRACTICE to make it the current directory.

3 In the Save Database As box, type **BONBOX05**

The DBF extension is added automatically.

4 Click the Save push button.

5 Click the Yes push button when you see the message asking whether you want to input records now.

Enter information in the new table

Enter the information shown on the following index card into your new table.

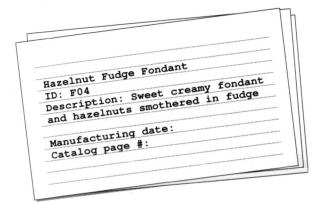

Close the active window

▶ Double-click the Control-menu box to close the window.

Even though you have closed the window in which you entered records into the BONBOX05 file, the file is still open. The status bar in the lower-left corner of the window displays the name of the open file.

Modifying the Table Structure

After reviewing the stack of index cards, you realize that the table structure does not match the information you need to enter. For example, you discover that one field needs to be longer, and you want to delete two other fields. In addition, by adding two new fields, you could track bonbon manufacturing information more accurately. By using FoxPro for Windows, you can easily adjust the table structure to meet your changing information requirements. Start by opening the table structure and making your changes in the Table Structure dialog.

Open the table structure

1   From the Database menu, choose Setup.

The Setup dialog appears.

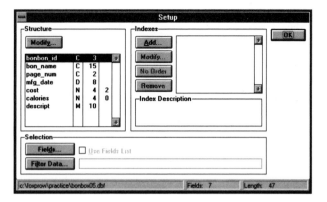

2 Click the Modify push button.

The Table Structure dialog appears.

Change the field length

The Name field is not long enough to include the complete name of some bonbons.

1 Click the number "15" in the Width column for the Bon_name field.

2 Click the up arrow on the spinner control until "25" appears in the field.

Insert two new fields

Using FoxPro for Windows, you can maintain more categories of information than you can in a paper-based system. Add two new fields so that Manufacturing can track the kind of chocolate and nuts used in each bonbon.

1 Click the Descript field, and then click the Insert push button.

A new field appears between the Calories field and the Descript field.

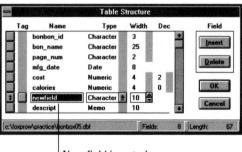

New field inserted

2 In the Name column, type **choc_type** to replace the current field name.

3 Press TAB to move to the Type column.

The correct field type, Character, is already selected.

4 Press TAB to move to the Width column.

5 Click the up arrow of the spinner control until "15" appears in the field.

6 Click the Insert push button to add another field.

7 In the Name column, type **nut_type**

8 Press TAB to move to the Type column.

The correct field type, Character, is already selected.

9 Press TAB to move to the Width column.

10 Click the up arrow of the spinner control until "15" appears in the field.

Delete a field

Because no one truly wants to know the number of calories in a bonbon, you decide to delete this field.

1 Click anywhere in the line for the Calories field.

2 Click the Delete push button.

The Calories field is removed from the list of fields.

Delete another field

Because Sweet Lil's is now producing several different catalogs every month, the page number field is no longer meaningful. You can delete this field as well.

1 Click anywhere in the line for the Page_num field.

2 Click the Delete push button.

The Page_num field is removed from the list of fields. The Table Structure dialog looks like the following illustration.

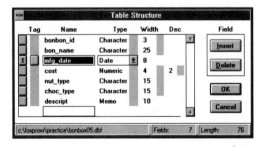

Rearranging Fields in a Table Structure

To make it easier to enter bonbon information, you can move the fields around in the structure. With the fields displayed in an order that more closely resembles the information on the 3" x 5" index cards, it will be easier to enter new records.

Rearrange fields

1 Drag the Mover button for the Mfg_date field to just above the Descript field.

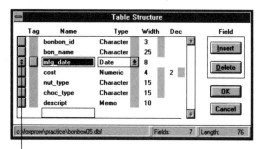

Drag the Mover button for the Mfg_date field.

2 Drag the Cost field to just above the Mfg_date field.

3 Click the OK push button to close the Table Structure dialog.

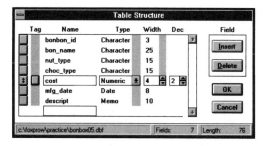

4 Click the Yes push button when you see the message asking whether you want to make these changes permanent.

5 Click the OK push button to close the Setup dialog.

One Step Further

Converting to a computer-based database system from an existing paper-based system is an excellent opportunity to re-evaluate your information requirements. Information that once seemed important might not be critical any longer. For example, as you examine the bonbon index cards, you notice that the Manufacturing date field on the cards seldom contains any information. You discuss this with the director of Manufacturing and learn that this information is not really important.

As you learned earlier in this book, the Command window displays the corresponding command for the selections you make from the menus. Although making menu selections is an easy way to get to the dialog you want, entering a command in the Command window is often a faster, more direct approach.

You can also simply enter the first four characters of each command:
MODI STRU

1   In the Command window, type **MODIFY STRUCTURE**

2   Press ENTER.

The Table Structure dialog appears. This is the same dialog you see when you select Setup from the Database menu and click the Modify push button in the Setup dialog.

3   Delete the Mfg_date field.

The director of Manufacturing also wants to keep track of the type of filling in each bonbon. Add a field to the table structure that will contain this information.

4   Click the Choc_type field, and then click the Insert push button to add a new field between the Choc_type and the Nut_type field.

5   Name the field **fill_type**, and give it the same specifications as the Nut_type field.

6   Click the OK push button to close the Table Structure dialog. Answer Yes when you see the message asking whether you want to make the changes permanent.

Entering Data Faster

Many of the bonbons that Sweet Lil's makes are quite similar to each other, differing only in the kind of chocolate, filling, or nut. To save time when entering records containing similar information, use the SET CARRY ON command in the Command window. Then when you choose the Append Record option, the contents of the last record are copied to the end of the file. Now you can edit the new records rather than type the records from scratch.

1   In the Command window, type **SET CARRY ON**

2   Press ENTER.

3   In the Command window, type **BROWSE**

4   Press ENTER.

You can also press CTRL+N to append new records to the file.

5   From the Browse menu, choose Append Record.

6   Edit the new record so that it contains information for the bonbon described on the card shown in the following illustration.

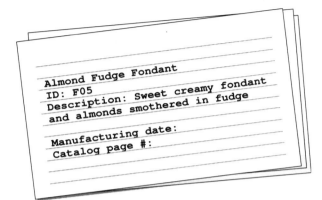

If You Want to Continue to the Next Lesson

1   From the Window menu, choose View.

2   In the View window, click the Close push button.

If You Want to Quit FoxPro for Windows for Now

▶   From the File menu, choose Exit.

Lesson Summary

To	Do this
Create a new table file	From the File menu, choose New. In the New dialog, click the Table/DBF radio button. When you click the New push button, the Table Structure dialog appears. Specify the fields in your table.
Add a field	In the Table Structure dialog, click the blank box in the Name column, and enter a field name.
Insert a field	In the Table Structure dialog, select the field below where you want. Click the Insert push button.
Delete a field	In the Table Structure dialog, select the field to delete. Click the Delete push button.
Modify the table structure	From the Database menu, choose Setup. Click the Modify push button, and make changes in the Table Structure dialog.

For more information on	See in *Microsoft FoxPro for Windows Getting Started*
Creating a table	Chapter 10, Working with Your Own Table
Table structure	Chapter 10, Working with Your Own Table

For more information on	See in the *Microsoft FoxPro for Windows User's Guide*
Field types	Chapter 2, File Menu (New)
Using the Setup dialog	Chapter 4, Database Menu Chapter 7, Window Menu (View)

For more information on	See in the *Microsoft FoxPro for Windows Language Reference*
Modify Structure command	Modify Structure
Set Carry command	Set Carry

Preview of the Next Lesson

Because you can connect tables with FoxPro for Windows, you can create several smaller tables, rather than a single large one. In the next lesson, you will learn how to use a query to obtain information stored in multiple tables.

Reporting with Many Tables in a Query

Sometimes the information you need is not found in a single table. Because FoxPro for Windows allows you to establish relationships between tables, you can gather all the information you need at once, even if the data is stored in several tables.

In this lesson, you will learn how to join tables by a field they have in common. Once this link is established, you can retrieve and report information from many tables at one time. You will also learn how to group data in a report and use advanced reporting techniques, such as creating bands and computed fields.

You will learn how to:

- Join multiple tables.
- Group data.
- Change band size.
- Create new fields on a report.
- Create computed fields.

Estimated lesson time: 40 minutes

If you closed FoxPro for Windows at the end of the last lesson

▶ Start FoxPro for Windows by double-clicking the FoxPro for Windows icon.

Connecting Multiple Tables

In this lesson, you will use a version of the bonbon table (BONBON) you created in the previous lesson. This table already contains dozens of records of the different bonbon types produced by Sweet Lil's. Some of the information you need is stored in this table; however, additional data you need is stored in two other tables: One table, called BOX, contains the detailed contents of Sweet Lil's collections of bonbons; the other table, called BOXES, contains summary information about the boxes on hand.

First, open and modify an existing query to join the BONBON table with the BOX table. Then, you can join a third table.

Open an existing query

1   From the File menu, choose Open.

The Open dialog appears.

2   In the List Files Of Type popup, select "Query."

3   In the Directory list, double-click PRACTICE to make it the current directory.

PRACTICE is already the current directory if you did not exit FoxPro for Windows at the end of the last lesson.

4   In the File Name list, select LSNQ06.QPR.

5   Click the Open push button.

The RQBE window appears.

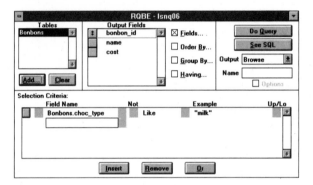

Save the query with a new name

Before you make any changes to this query, save the query with a new name. This leaves you with the original query unchanged, so you can repeat this lesson if you choose.

1   From the File menu, choose Save As.

The Save As dialog appears.

2   In the Save Current Document As box, type **SWEETQ06.QPR**

3   Click the Save push button.

Joining Tables

One way to relate tables is to join them from within a query. You simply specify the files you want to join, and then identify the field they have in common.

The query that you just opened selects records for bonbons made with milk chocolate and displays their bonbon ID, name, and cost. Because you also want to obtain information located in BOX.DBF and BOXES.DBF, you need to join all three tables.

Join two tables

1   In the Tables area of the RQBE window, click the Add push button.

Click here.

The Open dialog appears.

2   In the Select A Table list, double-click BOX.DBF.

The RQBE Join Condition dialog appears. The popups display the field that the tables have in common, bonbon_id. The field names in the Join Condition dialog and the RQBE window are *fully qualified*. This means that the field name is preceded by the name of the table to which the field belongs.

3   In the popup on the left, Box.bonbon_id is already selected.

4   In the popup on the right, Bonbons.bonbon_id is already selected.

5   Click the OK push button to return to the RQBE window.

BONBONS and BOX are now joined by the field they have in common, Bonbon_id.

The table name, BOX, now appears in the Tables area along with the BONBONS table. In the Selection Criteria area, the common fields are identified by the two-headed arrow on the left.

Joined tables

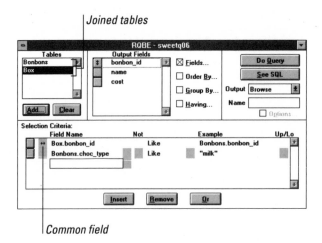

Common field

Join another table

1 In the Tables area of the RQBE window, click the Add push button.

The Open dialog appears.

2 In the Select A Table list, double-click BOXES.DBF.

The RQBE Join Condition dialog appears. The popups display the first field that the tables have in common. However, you can join the tables with any field they have in common.

3 In the RQBE Join Condition dialog, click the down arrow next to the popup on the left, and select Boxes.box_id.

4 Click the down arrow next to the popup on the right, and select Box.box_id.

5 Click the OK push button to return to the RQBE window.

Joined tables

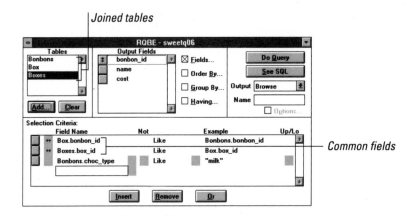

Common fields

BOXES.DBF and BOX.DBF are now joined by the field they have in common, Box_id. Once the tables are joined, you can select output fields and specify selection criteria from all three tables in the query.

Modifying the Query

Sweet Lil's Manufacturing department wants to know the names of the boxes that contain milk chocolate bonbons for which there are 400 or fewer boxes on hand, and the number of milk chocolate bonbons in each box. This information will help the Manufacturing department determine how many more of these boxes to produce to accommodate a big increase in sales projected for the next quarter.

Add output fields

In the Output Fields area, add the fields that contain the names and the quantity of the boxes from the BOXES table, and add the field that contains the quantity of bonbons in each box from the BOX table.

1   In the Output Fields area, click the Fields check box.

The RQBE Select Fields dialog appears.

2   In the RQBE Select Fields dialog, double-click the Boxes.box_name field from the Table Fields list.

You need to scroll through the list to find this field.

3   Double-click the Box.quantity from the Table Fields list.

4   Double-click Boxes.quantity from the Table Fields list.

Remove an output field

Because the director of Manufacturing does not want cost information in this query, you can remove the Cost field.

1   In the Selected Output list, double-click the Bonbons.cost field to remove it.

2   Click the OK push button.

Add a selection criterion

Add a selection criterion so that only those boxes for which there are 400 or fewer boxes on hand are displayed.

1   In the Selection Criteria area, click the blank box under Field Name.

A popup of field names appears. Fields from each table are separated by a line in the list.

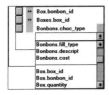

2   Select Boxes.quantity from the popup.

3   Click the field in the comparison operator column.

A popup of comparison operators appears.

4   Select Less Than from the popup.

5   In the Example column, type **401**

The RQBE window looks like the following illustration.

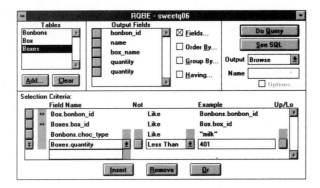

Do the query

▶   Click the Do Query push button to display the results of your query.

From BOXES table
From BOX table

Bonbon_id	Name	Box_name	Quantity_a	Quantity_b
M04	Peanut Butter Delight	Sweet Creams	6	200
M16	Marzipan Marvel	Heavenly Hazelnuts	3	300
M08	Marzipan Maple	Autumn Collection	6	200
M08	Marzipan Maple	Island Collection	6	400
M05	Marzipan Finch	Autumn Collection	6	200
M03	Pistachio Supreme	Supremes	2	400
M02	Macadamia Supreme	Supremes	2	400
M13	Sweet Marmalade	Sweet and Bitter	2	300
M09	Sweet Raspberry	Sweet and Bitter	2	300
M11	Sweet Cherry	Sweet and Bitter	2	300
M12	Sweet Blueberry	Sweet and Bitter	2	300
M12	Sweet Blueberry	Alpine Collection	4	400
M01	Sweet Strawberry	Sweet and Bitter	2	300
M01	Sweet Strawberry	Alpine Collection	5	400
M15	Tropical Palm	Heavenly Hazelnuts	2	300
M15	Tropical Palm	Island Collection	6	400
M06	Lover's Heart	Sweet Creams	6	200
M06	Lover's Heart	Lover's Hearts	4	300
M14	Hazelnut Cherry	Heavenly Hazelnuts	2	300

When fields from different tables have the same name, as in the case of the quantity fields from the BOX and BOXES tables, an _a, _b, _c notation is added to the field name, so you can tell them apart in the Browse window.

Close the Browse window

▶ Double-click the Control-menu box in the Browse window to close the window.

Save the query

▶ From the File menu, choose Save.

Displaying Data in a Report

This is exactly the information needed by the Manufacturing department to decide how many milk chocolate collections of bonbons to produce. In fact, this information would be valuable as a report to distribute at an upcoming department meeting.

In earlier lessons, you learned how to change the column title, add a title in the heading of the report, and format text. However, this data provides an opportunity to explore new ways to glean even more information from a report.

Grouping Data in a Report

Suppose you want a report to display a total of all the milk chocolate bonbons in a box. To display such information in your report, you need to create a *data grouping*. By grouping data, you can calculate totals, averages, and other summary data.

Create a report form

1　In the Output popup, select Report/Label.

2　Click the Options check box.

3　In the RQBE Display Options dialog, click the Report option push button.

4　Click the Quick Report check box.

The Quick Report dialog appears.

5　Click the OK push button to return to the RQBE Display Options dialog.

6　Click the OK push button to return to the RQBE dialog.

Do the query

1　Click the Do Query push button to display your query in Page Preview.

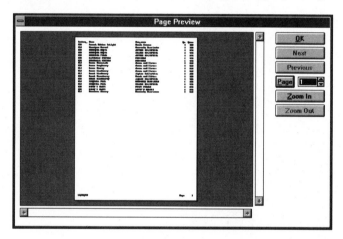

2　Click the OK push button to close the Page Preview window.

Open the report form

1　From the File menu, choose Open.

The Open dialog appears.

2　In the List Files Of Type popup, select Report.

3　Be sure PRACTICE is the current directory shown above the Directory list.

4　In the File Name list, select SWEETQ06.FRX.

5　Click the Open push button.

The Report Layout window for this report appears.

Group bonbon data

With a Report Layout window open, you can specify how you want to group the data. For example, to get a total of milk chocolates in each box, you need to group the records by the Box_name field from the BOXES table.

1   From the Report menu, choose Data Grouping.

The Data Grouping dialog appears.

2   Click the Add push button.

The Group Info dialog appears.

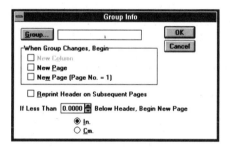

3   Click the Group push button.

The Expression Builder dialog appears.

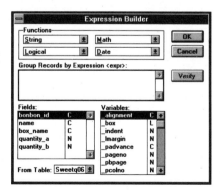

4 Click the From Table popup, and select Boxes.

5 In the Fields list, double-click Box_name.

This selection indicates that you want to group data by the box name field from the BOXES table. The Expression Builder dialog looks like the following illustration.

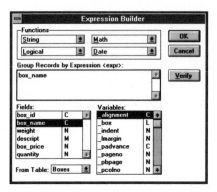

6 Click the OK push button to return to the Group Info dialog.

7 Verify that the New Page check box is cleared.

This selection indicates that you do not want each group of data to appear on separate pages.

Note If you have very large groups of data (for example, more than what could fit on a single page), you would check this box.

---

8 Click the OK push button to return to the Data Grouping dialog.

The Group box contains the field name you want to group (Box_name).

9 Click the OK push button to return to the Report Layout window.

Creating a Band of Data

The Report Layout window now contains another band in which you can specify and format information for your report. This area is the Group *band*. In the Report Layout window, the band is identified by the Group Header and Group Footer bars that include the name of the field you grouped. In our example, the Report Layout window displays Header and Footer bars for the Box_name group.

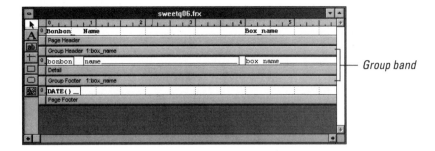

Group band

Changing Band Size

In the Group Footer band and Group Header band, you can insert fields that perform calculations on the group data. When you first add a group to the Report Layout window, the Group Footer and Detail bars are so close together that there is no space between them. Before you can insert a field, you need to increase the size of the band so that there is sufficient room for another field.

Increase the band size

▶ Be sure the horizontal scroll bar is all the way to the left. Drag the Sizing button for the Group Footer bar downward to the ¼-inch mark.

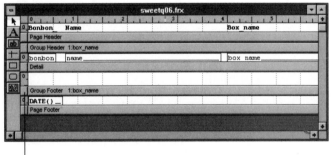

Drag the Group Footer bar to here.

Creating a Computed Field

To create a field that calculates data in a group, you first make a copy of the field containing the data to be calculated. After pasting and positioning the field where you want it to appear in the Group Footer band, you double-click the field to select the calculation you want to perform.

Copy and paste a field

Because you want to obtain a sum of the bonbons in each box, make a copy of the Quantity_a field.

1 In the Detail band, click the Quantity_a field.

You need to scroll to the right to see the field.

2 From the Edit menu, choose Copy.

3 From the Edit menu, choose Paste.

4 Drag the new field to the Group Footer band.

Try to align the field at the bottom edge of the band, below the Quantity_a field.

Tip To place the objects in the Report Layout window more precisely, turn off the Snap To Grid option.

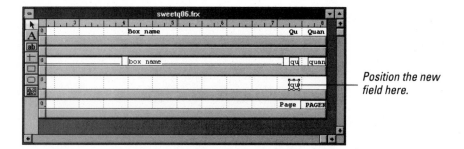

Position the new field here.

Assign a calculation to a field

1 Double-click the new field in the Group Footer band.

The Report Expression dialog appears.

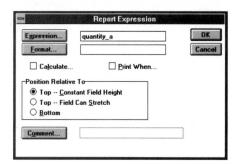

2 Click the Calculate check box.

The Calculate dialog appears.

3   Click the Sum radio button.

4   Click the OK push button.

5   In the Report Expression dialog, click the OK push button to return to the Report Layout window.

Creating Another Computed Field

You are not limited to a single field in the band for this group of data. Although the director of Manufacturing did not explicitly request this information, it might be useful to get the total of each type of milk chocolate bonbon allocated to a box. While you are doing so, you can also have the report calculate the total number of milk chocolate bonbons (regardless of type) allocated for all the boxes of each type.

Change the page orientation

Because you are adding new fields that will appear in a new column of the report, you need to change the orientation of the page to landscape, so that all the columns will fit across the width of the page.

1   From the Report menu, choose Page Layout.

2   In the Page Layout dialog, click the Print Setup push button.

3   In the Print Setup dialog, click the Landscape radio button.

4   Click the OK push button in each dialog until you return to the Report Layout window.

Create a new detail field

Add another calculated field to the Detail band that multiplies the number of bonbons by the number of boxes on hand. Rather than copy and paste an existing field, you can create a new field with the field tool.

1   Click the field tool.

2   In the Detail band, drag a box (of any size) just to the right of the Quantity_b field.

   When you release the mouse button, the Report Expression dialog appears.

Field tool

Assign a calculation to the field

1   Click the Expression push button.

2   In the Expression Builder dialog, double-click Quantity_a in the Fields list.

The field appears in the Expression For Field On Report area. The insertion point is positioned after the field.

3   Click the down arrow next to the Math popup to display a list of mathematical operations you can perform.

You can also simply type the appropriate operator to enter a simple mathematical operation.

4   Select *

The asterisk (the second selection in the list) represents the multiplication operation.

5   Double-click Quantity_b in the Fields list.

The field appears in the Expression For Field On Report area after the asterisk.

6   Click the OK push button to return to the Report Expression dialog.

7   Click the OK push button to return to the Report Layout window.

8   With the new field selected, resize the field until it is about two and a half squares wide.

Create a new Group Footer field

Add another calculated field in the Group Footer band to display a sum of the bonbons on hand per box.

1   With the new field still selected, from the Edit menu, choose Copy.

2   From the Edit menu, choose Paste.

3   Drag the new field to the Group Footer band.

Try to align the field at the bottom edge of the band, below the Quantity_a*Quantity_b field you created in the previous step.

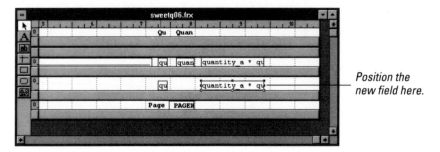

Position the new field here.

Assign a calculation to a field

1   Double-click the new field in the Group Footer band.

The Report Expression dialog appears.

2   Click the Calculate check box.

The Calculate dialog appears.

3   Click the Sum radio button.

4   Click the OK push button.

5   In the Report Expression dialog, click the OK push button to return to the Report Layout window.

6   Click the text tool.

7   Click to the right of the new field, and type **Milk Bonbons**

Preview the report

1   From the Report menu, choose Page Preview.

2   Click the text of the report to get a close-up view.

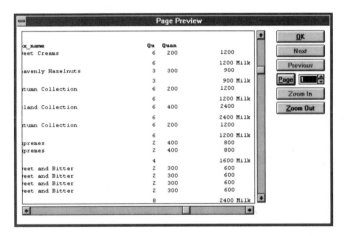

3   Click the OK push button to return to the Report Layout window.

Tip   If a column of data does not appear in the Page Preview window as you expected, it means that the column width specified in the Report Layout window is too narrow or that you positioned the column too close to the other columns. Return to the Report Layout window to adjust and reposition the columns.

Formatting the Report

Before distributing your report, you can use some of the formatting techniques you learned in Lesson 4 to make your report easier to read.

Draw a line

Separate the detail records from the Group band with lines over the total fields.

1   Click the line tool.

2   In the Group Footer band, draw a line above the Quantity_a field. Make the line as long as the field.

3   In the Group Footer band, draw a line above the Quantity_a*Quantity_b field. Make the line about as long as the field.

Add lines above the
Group Footer fields.

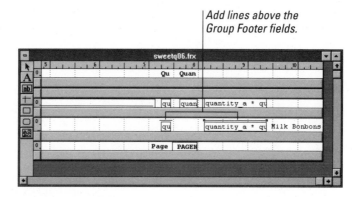

Format the new fields

1   With the pointer tool, select all the objects in the Group Footer band.

2   From the Object menu, choose Font.

3   In the Font Style box, select Bold.

4   Click the OK push button.

Increase space between groups

▶   Drag the Sizing button for Group Header bar downward to the 1/8-inch mark.

You may need to scroll the Report Layout window all the way to the left so that you can see the labels identifying the correct bar to move.

Preview the report

1   From the Report menu, choose Page Preview.

2   Click the text of the report to get a close-up view.

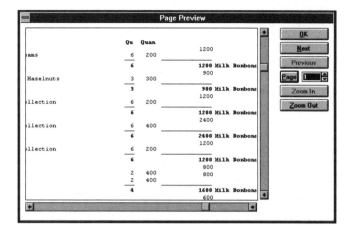

3   Click the OK push button to return to the Report Layout window.

Further

The report was a big success at the Manufacturing department meeting. So that each supervisor can have an accurate inventory, the director wants the report to contain the total number of bonbons for all the boxes on hand. This means you need to add a field to the report that contains the total number of bonbons. You can use the Expression Builder to make it easy to get grand totals for the entire report.

Create a report summary field

1   From the Report menu, choose Title/Summary.

The Title/Summary dialog appears.

2   Click the Summary Band check box, and click the OK push button.

3   In the Detail band, select, copy, and then paste the Quantity_a*Quantity_b field. Position the new field in the Summary band, aligning the field under Quantity_a*Quantity_b.

You may need to scroll downward to see the Summary band.

4 Double-click the field to display the Report Expression dialog.

5 Click the Calculate check box, and be sure the Sum radio button is selected.

6 Click the arrow to the right of the Reset popup to display a list of reset options, and verify that End Of Report is already selected.

7 Click the OK push button in each dialog until you return to the Report Layout window.

8 Click the text tool.

9 Click to the left of the new field, and type **Total Bonbons**

10 Scroll to the right until "Page" displays in the Page Footer band. With the pointer tool, select the Page and the PAGE() field, and drag them to the far right edge of the report (to about the 10-inch mark).

Preview the report

1 From the Report menu, choose Page Preview.

2 Click the text near the bottom of the report to get a close-up view of the Total Bonbons.

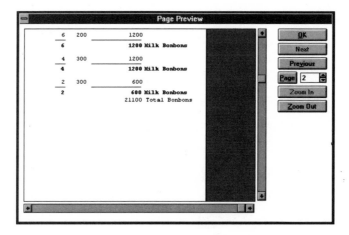

3 Click the OK push button to return to the Report Layout window.

Close the Report Layout window

1 Double-click the Control-menu box to close the Report Layout window.

2 Click the Yes push button when you see the message asking whether you want to save your changes.

Close the RQBE window

1 Double-click the Control-menu box to close the RQBE window.

2 Click the Yes push button when you see the message asking whether you want to save your changes.

If You Want to Continue to the Next Lesson

1 From the Window menu, choose Command.

2 In the Command window, type **close all**

3 Press ENTER.

The Close All command closes all windows and files which are open in all work areas.

4 Click the Yes button when you see the message asking whether you want to save your changes.

If You Want to Quit FoxPro for Windows for Now

▶ From the File menu, choose Exit.

Lesson Summary

To	Do this
Join tables	In the Tables area of the RQBE window, click the Add push button. In the Open dialog from the Select A Table list, double-click the name of the table you want to join. In the RQBE Join Condition dialog, select the common fields for both tables. Click the OK push button to return to the RQBE window.
Group data in a report	From the Report menu, choose Data Grouping. In the Data Grouping dialog, click the Add push button. In the Group Info dialog, click the Group push button. In the Expression Builder dialog, click the From Table popup, and select the table containing the field you want to group. In the Fields list, double-click the field name by which you want to group the data.
Change the band size	Drag the Sizing button (to the left of the bar you want to move).
Create a new field with the field tool	Click the field tool. Drag a box where you want the new field to be. When you release the mouse button, the Report Expression dialog appears. Click the Expression push button. In the Expression Builder dialog, double-click the field in the Fields list that you want for the new field.

To	Do this
Assign a calculation to a field	Double-click the new field. In the Report Expression dialog, click the Calculate check box. In the Calculate dialog, click the calculation option you want.

For more information on	See in *Microsoft FoxPro for Windows Getting Started*
Querying with multiple tables	Chapter 2, Quick Start Chapter 7, Reporting with Multiple Tables
Grouping data and creating bands in a report	Chapter 7, Reporting with Multiple Tables

For more information on	See in the *Microsoft FoxPro for Windows User's Guide*
Calculated fields	Chapter 4, Database Menu
Join conditions	Chapter 13, Querying Your Data with RQBE
Creating bands in a report	Chapter 14, Designing Reports and Labels

Preview of the Next Lesson

In the next lesson, you will learn how you can improve the organization of the data stored in the table by using indexing. Indexing allows you to order the records in a table so that you can retrieve information quickly—without taking up valuable disk storage space.

Sorting and Indexing

You are already familiar with ordering records by a field when using a query. But if you need to modify records that you also want to display in a specific order, ordering records in a query is not a feasible solution.

In this lesson, you will learn about the two ways to order records in a table. To understand the differences between sorting and indexing, you will first sort a table. Next you will create several index keys in an index file. After modifying an existing index file and creating index keys based on multiple field expressions, you will use the Seek option to locate specific records.

You will learn how to:

- Sort a table.
- Create a structural compound index.
- Modify an existing index.
- Search for specific records using the Seek option.

Estimated lesson time: 45 minutes

If you closed FoxPro for Windows at the end of the last lesson

▶ Start FoxPro for Windows by double-clicking the FoxPro for Windows icon.

Open the ORDERS table

The Orders table contains information for about 400 orders made by Sweet Lil's customers.

1 From the Window menu, choose View.

2 In the View window, click the Open push button.

The Open dialog appears.

3 In the Directory list, double-click PRACTICE to make it the current directory.

PRACTICE is already the current directory if you did not exit FoxPro for Windows at the end of the last lesson.

4 In the Select A Table list, select the table called ORDERS.DBF.

5 Click the Open push button.

6 Click the Browse push button.

Sorting a Table

After using the ORDERS table for a while, the Customer Service department observed that it would be easier to enter and maintain order information if the records were sorted by customer ID. As the PC Support manager, you have been asked to organize the ORDERS table so that Sweet Lil's Customer Service department can work more efficiently.

One way you can order records in a table is with the Sort option.

Sort the ORDERS table

When you sort a table, you are actually creating another table. This new table has the same records and information as the original table, but the records are sorted in the manner you specify.

1 From the Database menu, choose Sort.

The Sort dialog appears.

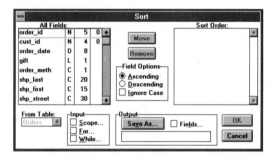

Double-clicking a field in the All Fields list is the same as selecting the field you want and clicking the Move push button.

2 In the All Fields list, double-click Cust_id.

3 In the Output area, click the Save As push button.

The Save As dialog appears.

4 In the Sort Destination File box, type **ORDRSRT**

Be sure PRACTICE is the current directory shown above the Directory list.

5 Click the Save push button to return to the Sort dialog.

Because you want this sorted file to contain the same fields as the ORDERS file, do not click the Fields check box. Unless you specify differently, all the fields are automatically copied into the new table.

6 Click the OK push button.

Because you are still in the ORDERS table, you will not see any change to the table in the Browse window.

7 Minimize the Browse window.

You will return to this window later in this lesson.

Open the sorted table

1 In the View window, select Work Area 2.

2 Click the Open push button.

3 In the Select A Table list, select the table called ORDRSRT.DBF.

Be sure PRACTICE is the current directory shown above the Directory list.

4 Click the Open push button.

The View window indicates ORDERS is open is Work Area 1 and ORDRSRT is open in Work Area 2 (the current work area).

Browse through the sorted table

▶ With Work Area 2 still selected, click the Browse push button.

The new table appears in the Browse window. The records are sorted by the Cust_id field.

Order_id	Cust_id	Order_date	Gift	Order_meth	Shp_last	Shp_first
6	1	02/06/92	T	P	Kahn	Juliet
300	1	09/09/92	F	P	Carter	Rita
214	2	07/06/92	T	P	Adams	Cathy
363	2	10/23/92	T	P	Adams	Cathy
345	3	10/11/92	T	P	Fuller	Sandy
141	4	05/14/92	F	M	Kemper	Wally
26	5	02/20/92	T	P	Tilton	Lester
10	7	02/09/92	F	P	Meese	Albert
308	8	09/16/92	F	P	Goudie	Arlene
196	10	06/25/92	T	P	Fuller	Sandy
76	11	03/29/92	T	P	Hayes	Susan
288	12	08/30/92	F	P	Swaggert	Tom
299	13	09/08/92	F	P	Hernandez	Jim
379	13	11/06/92	F	P	Hernandez	Jim
368	14	10/27/92	T	P	Rice	Jennifer
290	15	08/31/92	F	P	Magruder	Roberta

Sorting Considerations

Because you are creating another version of a table when you sort, keep in mind the following file management and maintenance issues before using the Sort option:

- Duplicate files take up valuable disk space on your computer.

- Having multiple copies of the same data means you have to remember to update all files whenever you make a change in one file. Remembering to maintain multiple files is not a reliable way to store important data.

- It can be difficult to determine whether a file has been properly updated and which file contains the most current data.

Close the sorted table

1 In the Browse window, double-click the Control-menu box.

2   With Work Area 2 still selected, click the Close push button.

The View window indicates ORDERS is still open in Work Area 1.

Understanding Indexing

Indexing is another way to order records in a table so that you can retrieve information quickly. Because indexing does not create a duplicate table, you can order records in as many ways as you want without creating a maintenance nightmare.

When you index a table, the records in the table are not physically rearranged (as they are when you sort a table). Instead, indexing creates an *index file* associated with the table. An index file is a list of entries that identifies the different ways you want to order a table. In addition, because an index file does not contain database data, it is much smaller than an entire table, so you save disk space, too.

Creating a Structural Compound Index

A *structural compound index* is an index file that has the same name as the table, but the name has a CDX extension. When you open a table that has a structural compound index, its index file opens at the same time. When you make a change to the table, all of its open index files are also updated. You create a structural compound index file by opening the Setup dialog for the table you want to index. Then you enter an index specification, known as an *index key*. A structural compound index is the default for the type of index you can create.

Note   You can create other types of index files, including files that have different names from the table and are not automatically opened and updated with the original table. These other index files are often used in extremely large database applications to create temporary index files or to create files compatible with other database software. Refer to the FoxPro for Windows documentation for additional information.

Open the Setup dialog for a table

You can open the Setup dialog from the View window.

1   Select ORDERS in Work Area 1.

2   In the View window, click the Setup push button.

The Setup dialog appears.

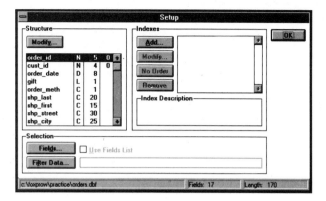

Adding an Index Key

You learned how to use the Setup dialog when you modified a table structure. You use the same dialog to create index keys that specify how you want to index your table.

Add an index key field

Create an index key to order records by state.

1   In the Indexes area of the Setup dialog, click the Add push button.

The Open dialog appears. Be sure PRACTICE is the current directory shown above the Directory list.

2   Click the New push button.

The Index dialog appears.

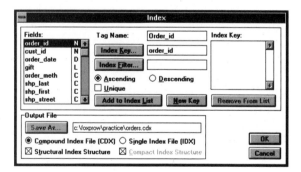

3   Select the Shp_state field in the Fields list.

Shp_state appears in the Tag Name field. The *tag name* is the name for this index key. Whenever you refer to a particular index key, you can use its tag name. The field name is automatically supplied as the tag name, but you can change the tag name if you want.

4   Click the Add To Index List push button.

The Shp_state field appears in the Index Key list. This index key orders the table records by state.

Add another index key field

You can specify multiple index keys to be included in the index file. To have the ability to order the records by city, for example, specify Shp_city as another index key.

Double-clicking the field is the same as selecting the field you want and clicking the Add To Index List push button.

▶   Double-click Shp_city to add it to the Index Key list.

Even though you may not see it appear in the Tag Name box, a tag name is supplied for this index key that is the same as the field name, Shp_city.

Specifying Order

When you add a field to the Index Key list, FoxPro for Windows places an up arrow next to the field name. This arrow indicates that the records will be displayed in ascending order (A to Z, 0 to 9). By clicking the Descending radio button, you can specify that you want the records displayed in descending order (9 to 0, Z to A). A down arrow indicates descending order.

Specify descending order

1   In the Index Key list, select Shp_state.

2   Click the Descending radio button.

The arrow next to the field now points downward, indicating that records ordered by this field will be displayed in descending order.

Descending order index key

3   Click the OK push button to return to the Setup dialog.

Browsing Through the Indexed Table

Now that you have specified a few different index keys, you must choose the order by which you want the records displayed in the Browse window. For example, to display records in ascending order by city, you select the Orders: Shp_city tag name from the Indexes list, and click the Set Order push button.

Verify the display order

1   In the Indexes list, select Orders: Shp_city.

When an order is set, a small key appears next to the tag name in the Indexes list. FoxPro for Windows automatically sets the order to the last key you created.

Order set to Shp_city

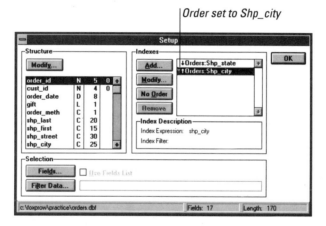

2   Click the OK push button to return to the View window.

Browse through the table

1   Click the Browse push button.

The Browse window displays the records in ascending order by city. You may need to scroll the window to the right to see the Shp_city field.

2   Double-click the Control-menu box to close the Browse window.

Establish a new display order

1   In the View window, click the Setup push button.

The Setup dialog appears.

2   In the Indexes list, select Orders: Shp_state.

3 Click the Set Order push button.

A key appears next to the Shp_state tag.

4 Click the OK push button to return to the View window.

Browse through the table

▶ Click the Browse push button.

Your Browse window displays the records in descending order by state.

Searching for Records Using Seek

Now that you have ordered your table using a tag, you can find records that match specific criteria. In earlier lessons, you used the Locate option to specify search criteria. With an indexed table, you can also use the Seek option. This option allows you to specify a search criterion based on the index key that is currently set. Although you can still use the Locate option, the Seek option works faster, because it uses the index key when searching in an indexed table. For tables containing thousands of records, speed can be an important consideration.

Search for a record

Suppose you want to work with the records for orders shipped to California. Use the Seek option to move to the first record containing CA in the Shp_state field.

1 From the Record menu, choose Seek.

The Expression Builder dialog appears.

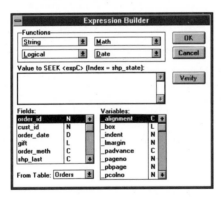

2 In the Value To Seek box, type **"CA"**

Be sure to enter the quotation marks before and after the value.

Because your search criterion is restricted to the field specified in the index key identified as the current sort order, you need only enter the value for which you want to search, not the complete field expression as you do with the Locate option.

3 Click the OK push button.

The first record that has CA in the Shp_state field appears as the current record in the Browse window.

4 Double-click the Control-menu box to close the Browse window.

Modifying an Existing Index

As indicated earlier, you can have many index keys in an index file. You can modify an index file (add, remove, and change index keys) by clicking the Modify push button in the Setup dialog.

Open the Index dialog

1 In the View window, click the Setup push button.

The Setup dialog appears.

2 In the Indexes area, click the Modify push button.

The Index dialog appears.

Creating a Multiple Field Expression Index Key

You are not limited to ordering by a single field. For example, if you want to display records ordered by state and then by city within each state, you can create an index expression to order records by both fields. With the aid of the Expression Builder, you can specify the expression for creating multiple field index keys.

Create another index key

Add an index key based on a multiple field expression.

1 Click the New Key push button.

2 Click the Index Key push button.

The Expression Builder dialog appears.

3 In the Fields list, double-click Shp_state.

The Shp_state field appears in the INDEX ON area. The insertion point is located after the field name.

4 Type a plus sign (+).

5 In the Fields list, double-click Shp_city.

The Shp_city field appears in the INDEX ON area after the plus sign. The Expression Builder dialog looks like the following illustration.

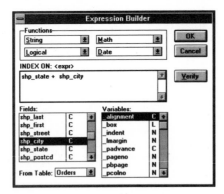

6   Click the OK push button to return to the Index dialog.

In the Index dialog, the box next to the Index Key push button displays the index expression you just created.

Creating a Tag Name

When you create an index key based on a single field expression, FoxPro for Windows supplies a tag name that is the same as the field name. When you create an index key for a multiple field expression, you must create your own unique tag name.

Enter a tag name

1   In the Tag Name box, type **Statecity**

2   Click the Add To Index List push button.

3   Click the OK push button.

The Setup dialog appears.

The new tag appears in the Indexes list with a key next to it, indicating this is the current sort order. The details of the selected index key appear in the Index Description area.

4   Click the OK push button.

Browse through the table

▶   In the View window, click the Browse push button.

The Browse window displays the records ordered by state and then by city within each state.

Using Seek in a Multiple Field Expression Index

Specifying search criteria for records ordered by a multiple field expression requires slightly different procedures than when seeking in a table ordered by a single field index key. This is because the multiple field expression is treated as a single, large field. For example, the expression for the Statecity tag, Shp_state + Shp_city, in effect combines the contents of the two fields before ordering the records.

When you want to use the Seek option to search for a specific record based on the contents of the second field in the expression, you must take into account the entire contents of both fields. This means you must anticipate any spaces between the contents of the first and second fields. For example, suppose you want to locate the first record for an order shipped to San Francisco. Use the following illustration to understand how FoxPro for Windows examines the contents of a multiple field expression to evaluate whether a record matches your criteria. If you want to search for the first record in which the Shp_city field contains San Francisco, your search criteria also needs to specify what the first field (Shp_state) in the expression needs to contain.

| C|A| | | | | | | | | | S|a|n| |F|r|a|n|c|i| |s|c|o| | | | | | | | | | | |

Shp_state
(Field length = 10)

Shp_city
(Field length = 25)

Using a Function

So that you do not have to count and enter the spaces yourself, you can use a function that supplies the spaces needed to make up the difference between the length of the text and the length of the field. Before you use a function with the Seek option, a little background about using functions in general will be helpful.

A *function* is a special command that provides a value. The value it provides depends on what the particular function is intended to do. There are many functions you can use. There are functions to convert one data type to another, to change text to upper-case, to perform calculations, even to tell you on which day of the week a specific date will fall. You can use functions in combination with many options and features in FoxPro for Windows. A function is characterized by the parentheses following the function name, such as PADR(). To use a function, you often need to enter additional information (known as *arguments*) within the parentheses that indicate how you want the function to work, such as PADR(CA, 10). In this expression, "CA" and "10" are the arguments.

The function you need when searching in a multiple field index key is called PADR(). It means "pad right," because this function provides a string of characters that includes the contents of the field, followed by the spaces required to fill the field.

Use a function with the Seek option

Suppose you want to search for the first order shipped to San Francisco, California. You need to use the PADR() function, with the text "CA" as the first argument and the field size as the second argument. Together, these arguments represent the value of the first field. This value combined with the value of the second field, "San Francisco," will allow you to locate the first order shipped to San Francisco.

1   From the Record menu, choose Seek.

The Expression Builder dialog appears.

2   In the Functions area, click the String popup to display string functions.

Recall that Shp_state is a character field. You need to use a string function to work with character fields.

3   Scroll to and select PADR(expC).

The function appears in the Value To Seek area of the Expression Builder dialog.

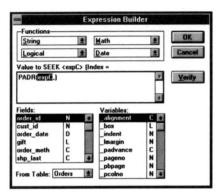

Note   Functions in the Expression Builder dialog are displayed with placeholder text inside the parentheses. This placeholder text represents the type of data the function requires as an argument. For example, "expC" means you must supply a character or string expression as an argument; "expN" represents a numeric expression; "expD" represents a date expression. When you enter an argument, the selected placeholder text is replaced by what you type.

4   With the insertion point inside the parentheses, type **"CA"**

Your typing replaces the placeholder text. This entry represents the first argument in the function.

5   Move the insertion point to the right of the comma, and type **10**

This is the size of the field, the second argument for PADR() function.

6 Move the insertion point to the right of the right parenthesis, and type **+ "San Fran"**

This is the value you want the second field to contain. You only need to enter enough text to make the search string unique. The Expression Builder dialog looks like the following illustration.

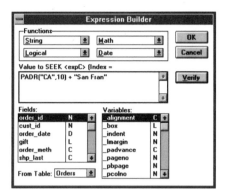

7 Click the Verify push button to make sure the expression is valid.

The message "Expression is valid" appears in the status bar. The expression searches for records in which the Shp_state field contains "CA," padded with spaces to fill the field, and also contains "San Fran" in the Shp_city field.

8 Click the OK push button to search for the first record that matches these criteria.

9 Double-click the Control-menu box to close the Browse window.

One Step Further

In this lesson, you learned to create an index key based on a multiple field expression. But there is a catch: The fields in the expression must be of the same type. That is, they must all be character fields, or date fields, or numeric fields. If you want to create a multiple field index key based on fields of differing types, you must use functions that convert the current data types so that all the fields are of the same type. Frequently used functions allow you to convert a date value to a character value, or a numeric value to a character value, or a character value to a numeric value. Such functions allow you to order the records the way you want. When converting values for use in an index key, you usually convert them to string or character values.

Suppose the Customer Service department has asked you to research and correct information about orders made in November. They have given you order forms (from which you will work) that have been organized by date. Each form contains the customer ID, along with the corrections to the orders you need to make. To help you complete this task, create an index key that orders the table first by order date (a date field) and then by customer ID (a numeric field.) Use functions to convert the values in both fields to strings.

Create a multiple field expression index key

1   In the View window, click the Setup push button.

2   In the Setup dialog, click the Modify push button in the Indexes area.

3   In the Index dialog, click the New Key push button.

4   Click the Index Key push button.

The Expression Builder dialog appears.

5   In the Functions area, click the Date popup to display the date functions.

A similar function, DTOC(), also converts a date value to a character value, but it does not use the format you need in an index key.

6   Scroll to and select DTOS(expD).

This function converts a date to a string. The function appears in the INDEX ON area.

7   With the insertion point inside the parentheses, double-click Order_date in the Fields list.

The Order_date replaces the expD placeholder text.

8   After the right parenthesis, type +

9   In the Functions area, click the String popup to display the string functions.

10   Scroll to and select STR(expN,,).

This function converts a number to a string. The function appears in the INDEX ON area after the plus sign.

11   In the Fields list, double-click Cust_id.

The Cust_id field replaces the expN placeholder text.

12   Press DEL twice to remove the extra commas that represent optional arguments.

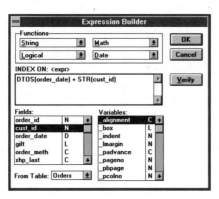

13   Click the Verify push button to make sure the expression is valid.

14   Click the OK push button to return to the Index dialog.

Create a new tag name

1 In the Tag Name box, type **Datecustid**

2 Click the Add To Index List push button, and then click the OK push button.

FoxPro for Windows returns to the Setup dialog. The new tag appears in the Indexes list with the order set to this tag.

3 Click the OK push button.

Browse the table

▶ In the View window, click the Browse push button.

The Browse window displays the records ordered by date and then by customer for each day.

Seek a record

Use the Seek option to move to the first record that has an order date of 11/15/92.

1 From the Record menu, choose Seek.

2 In the Expression Builder Functions area, scroll to and select DTOS(expD) in the Date popup.

Because you used this function in the index key, you need to include the function when you want to seek on a date. The function appears in the INDEX ON area of the Expression Builder dialog.

3 With the insertion point after the left parenthesis, type **{11/15/92}**

If you want to use a specific date, known as a *date constant*, you need to enclose the date in curly braces.

4 Click the OK push button to display the Browse window.

The record number appears for the date you specified.

Now you can work with the records for a particular date without having to scroll through the table. The customer ID records for each date are displayed in ascending order.

If You Want to Continue to the Next Lesson

1 From the Window menu, choose Command.

2 In the Command window, type **close all**

3 Press ENTER.

The Close All command closes all windows and files which are open in all work areas.

4 Click the Yes push button when you see the message asking whether you want to save your changes.

If You Want to Quit FoxPro for Windows for Now

▶ From the File menu, choose Exit.

Lesson Summary

To	Do this
Sort a table	Open the table you want to sort. From the Database menu, choose Sort. In the Sort dialog, double-click Cust_id in the All Fields list. In the Output area, click the Save As push button. In the Sort Destination File box, enter a new filename for the sort file. Click the OK push button. Click the Save push button to return to the Sort dialog. Click the Fields check box if you want the new table to contain a subset of the fields found in the original table. Click the OK push button.
Create a structural compound index	Open the table you want to index. From the Window menu, choose View. Click the Setup push button to display the Setup dialog. Add an index key field by clicking the Add push button in the Indexes area. In the Open dialog, click the New push button. In the Index dialog, select the field by which you want to index from the Fields list. Enter a new tag name in the Tag Name field if you want a different tag name. Click the Add To Index List push button.
Specify a descending order	In the Index Key list, select the field you want to order. Click the Descending radio button in the Setup dialog.
Specify an ascending order	In the Index Key list, select the field you want to order. Click the Ascending radio button in the Setup dialog.
Establish the display order	In the Indexes list, select the tag name for the index key you want. Click the Set Order push button. Click the OK push button to return to the View window.
Search for a record with Seek	Open the Browse window. From the Record menu, choose Seek. In the Expression Builder dialog, enter your search criteria. It must be the same as the index key specified in the current Sort Order. Enclose text values in quotation marks (" "); enclose date values in curly braces, { }.
Fill field spaces in an expression	Select the PADR() function in the Expression Builder dialog Functions area. Use a text value as the first argument, and use the number of characters needed to fill the field as the second argument.

To	Do this
Convert a date field to a character in an expression	Select the DTOS() function in the Expression Builder Functions area. Use the date field name as the argument.
Convert a date constant to a character in an expression	Select the DTOS() function in the Expression Builder Functions area. Use a specific date enclosed in curly braces as the argument.

For more information on	See in the *Microsoft FoxPro for Windows User's Guide*
Sorting	Chapter 4, Database Menu (Report)
Indexing	Chapter 4, Database Menu (Setup)

Preview of the Next Lesson

You may recall that you cannot modify records displayed for tables related in a query. In the next lesson, you will learn how to relate tables in the View window so that you can modify the records.

Relating Tables in the View Window

In this lesson, you will learn how to establish two different kinds of relationships using the View window. Unlike relating tables in a query, this method allows you to modify the records displayed in the Browse window. After using an example report to compare the one-to-one and one-to-many relationships, you will relate additional tables and use commands in the Command window to display fields from multiple tables at once. Finally, you will save this relationship information in a view file for easy retrieval later.

You will learn how to:

- Relate tables in a one-to-one relationship.
- Relate tables in a one-to-many relationship.
- Use the Browse Fields command in the Command window.
- Save View window settings in a view file.

Estimated lesson time: 50 minutes

If you closed FoxPro for Windows at the end of the last lesson

▶ Start FoxPro for Windows by double-clicking the FoxPro for Windows icon.

Using the View Window to Relate Tables

Sweet Lil's Marketing department has announced the winner of the Chocolate Lover of the Month recipe contest. With only the first and last name of the winning customer, your task is to modify an order to give the winner two free boxes of chocolates. Because you do not know the customer ID or order ID, you need to look up the name in the CUSTOMER table. Once you know the customer ID, you can modify order information in the ORDERS table. To have information from these tables available at the same time, you need to relate the tables.

When you relate tables using the RQBE window, you can display records to examine and report information. However, this information is *read-only*, which means you cannot change the information displayed. Although querying in multiple tables is a useful feature, it does not allow you to work with multiple tables when you need to edit them. Even though you could open separate work areas, this would require trying to find information in two separate Browse windows. If you are working with many records, relating tables in the View window is the solution.

Understanding Sweet Lil's Database Relationships

A database is a group of related tables. In this lesson, you will establish relationships among several tables, some of which you have already used in this book. Use the following list to keep track of the tables you work with in this lesson. This list also identifies the ID fields by which you can establish table relationships. The illustration that follows is a graphical representation of the relationships between tables.

Table	Description
CUSTOMER	Contains information about Sweet Lil's customers, including subscriptions to *The Chocolate Gourmet*. The Cust_id field identifies customers by a number. Each customer can have many orders.
ORDERS	Contains *summary* information about customer orders, including the shipping address and billing information. The Cust_id field identifies which customer placed the order. The Order_id field identifies the order number for an individual order. Each order can contain multiple items, but only one shipping destination, or one billing specification.
ORDER	Contains *detail* information about customer orders, including the item ordered and number of each item ordered. The Order_id field identifies the order to which the requested items belong. The Box_id field identifies the collection of bonbons ordered. Each order entry can contain multiple boxes.
BOXES	Contains *summary* information about a specific box of bonbons, including the weight, retail price, and the total number of this box on hand. The Box_id field identifies the box code for a box of bonbons.
BOX	Contains *detail* information about the contents of a box, including the quantity of each type of bonbon in the box. The Box_id field identifies the bonbon collection. The Bonbon_id field identifies the bonbon in the box. Each box can contain many different kinds of bonbons.
BONBONS	Contains specific information about individual bonbons, including the cost and ingredients. The Bonbon_id field identifies the bonbon with a code.

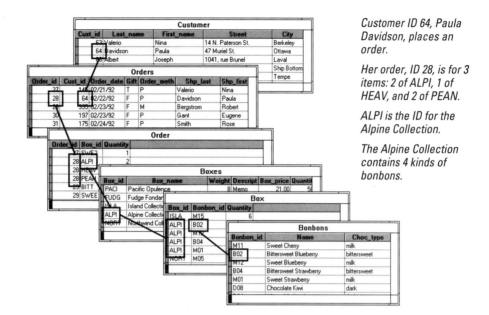

Customer ID 64, Paula Davidson, places an order.

Her order, ID 28, is for 3 items: 2 of ALPI, 1 of HEAV, and 2 of PEAN.

ALPI is the ID for the Alpine Collection.

The Alpine Collection contains 4 kinds of bonbons.

Establishing Relationships in the View Window

To relate tables in the View window, you establish relationships between two or more tables. You can relate tables in a one-to-one relationship (for example, for every customer there is one subscription record) or in a one-to-many relationship (for example, for every customer there are multiple order records). Before you can establish a one-to-many relationship, you must establish a one-to-one relationship first.

The first table is called the *parent* table, because it controls the relationship to the tables related to it. These other tables are called *child* tables. Table relationships are based on the common field between the parent and child tables. This field must be the index key of the current sort order of the child table. When you select a record in the parent table, the corresponding record in the child table (the one with the same value in the index key field) is also selected.

First, open the tables you want to relate. Then create a new index key, and set the sort order in the child table.

Open two tables

1   From the Window menu, choose View.

2   In the View window, click the Open push button.

The Open dialog appears.

3   In the Directory list, double-click PRACTICE to make it the current directory.

PRACTICE is already the current directory if you did not exit FoxPro for Windows at the end of the last lesson.

4   In the Select A Table list, select CUSTOMER.DBF.

5   Click the Open push button.

Double-clicking is the same as selecting the work area and clicking the Open push button to display the Open dialog.

6   In the View window, double-click Work Area 2.

7   In the Select A Table list, select ORDERS.DBF.

8   Click the Open push button.

Now both tables are open. CUSTOMER.DBF is open in Work Area 1, and ORDERS.DBF is open in Work Area 2.

Creating an Index Key in the Child Table

The CUSTOMER and the ORDERS tables have the Cust_id field in common. The ORDERS table must be indexed on this field. Before you begin, be sure Work Area 2 is still selected.

Add another index key field

The ORDERS table already has an index file associated with it. So that you can relate the ORDERS table to the CUSTOMER table, you need to add another index key to the index file.

1   In the View window, click the Setup push button.

The Setup dialog appears.

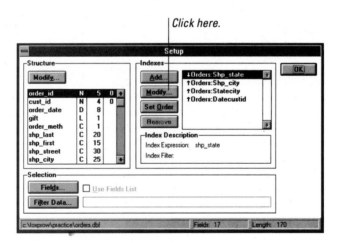

Click here.

2   In the Indexes area, click the Modify push button.

The Index dialog appears.

Click here.

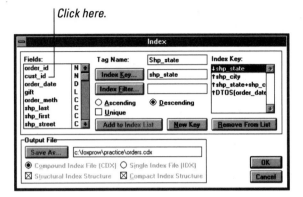

3 In the Fields list, select Cust_id.

4 Click the Ascending radio button.

5 Click the Add To Index List push button.

The Cust_id field appears in the Index Key list. This index key orders the records by customer ID.

6 Click the OK push button to return to the Setup dialog.

Be sure a small key appears next to the tag name "Orders: Cust_id" in the Indexes list, indicating the sort order is set to this new tag.

Sort order set to Cust_id.

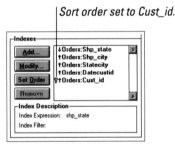

7 Click the OK push button to return to the View window.

Relating Tables One-to-One

One way tables can be related to each other is in a one-to-one relationship. This means that for every record in one table, there is no more than one corresponding record in a related table. For example, for every subscriber record there is only one customer record; similarly, every customer has no more than one subscription. You must establish a one-to-one relationship between tables before you can specify a one-to-many relationship for the tables.

Establish a one-to-one relationship

In the View window, you can establish relationships between any open tables. First you select the parent table. After you click the Relations push button, you select the table for this relationship.

1   In the View window, select CUSTOMER in Work Area 1.

2   Click the Relations push button.

The View window looks like the following illustration.

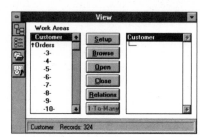

3   In the View window, select ORDERS in Work Area 2.

The Expression Builder dialog appears, indicating the common field by which the two tables can be related.

4   Click the OK push button to return to the View window.

The View window looks like the following illustration.

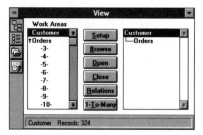

Generate a report

To better illustrate the results of relating these tables, generate a report that displays fields and records from both tables. Use a report form provided on the exercise disk.

1   From the Database menu, choose Report.

The Report dialog appears.

2   Click the Form push button.

The Open dialog appears.

3 In the Report File list, select LSNR08MD.FRX.

Be sure PRACTICE is the current directory shown above the Directory list.

4 Click the Open push button.

5 Click the OK push button.

The report appears in the Page Preview window.

Preview the report

1 Click the text of the report to get a close-up view.

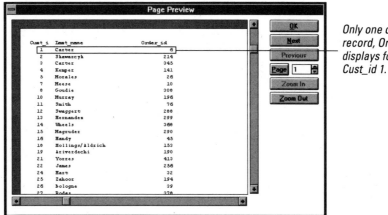

Only one order record, Order_id 6, displays for Cust_id 1.

This report displays only one order record for each customer ID. For example, for the customer ID 1, you see only order ID 6.

2 Click the OK push button to close the Page Preview window.

Browse through the table

Suppose you know that customer ID 1, Rita Carter, has made another order. You can verify the contents of the ORDERS table in the Browse window.

1 In the View window, select ORDERS in Work Area 2.

2 Click the Browse push button.

There are two order records for Cust_id 1.

Compare this Browse window to the report generated in the previous step. The report displayed only the first order record for each customer ID. However, the Browse window shows that Cust_id 1, Rita Carter, has made another order, Order_id 300. This order appears in the table but not in the report.

3   Close the Browse window.

In one-to-one relationships, the first record in the child table displays that matches the common field in the parent table. Then the next record in the parent table displays along with the first corresponding record in the child table.

Relating Tables One-to-Many

Another way that tables can be related to each other is in a one-to-many relationship. This means that for every record in the parent table, there can be many corresponding records in the child table. For example, for every customer there can be many orders.

In the previous step, we saw only one order record for each customer in the report but saw multiple order records for each customer in the ORDERS table itself. Because a one-to-one relationship does not reflect the fact that there are multiple orders per customer, you need to establish a one-to-many relationship between these two tables. Now that you have established an initial, one-to-one relationship between these two tables, you can change this relationship to a one-to-many relationship.

Tip   You must establish a one-to-one relationship before you can change it to a one-to-many relationship.

Establish a one-to-many relationship

1   In the View window, select CUSTOMER in Work Area 1.

2   Click the 1-To-Many push button.

The 1-To-Many dialog appears.

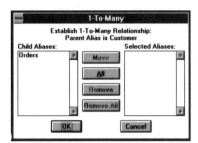

3   In the Child Aliases list, select "Orders."

4   Click the Move push button.

5   Click the OK push button.

The View window looks like the following illustration.

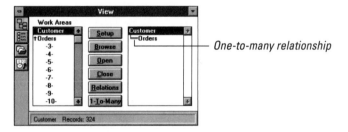

One-to-many relationship

Generate a report

To better illustrate the results of relating these tables in a one-to-many relationship, generate a report that displays fields from both tables. You can use the same report form you used in the previous exercise.

1   From the Database menu, choose Report.

2   In the Report dialog, click the Form push button.

The Open dialog appears.

3   In the Report File list, select LSNR08MD.FRX.

4   Click the Open push button.

5   Click the OK push button.

The report appears in the Page Preview window.

Preview the report

1   Click the text of the report to get a close-up view.

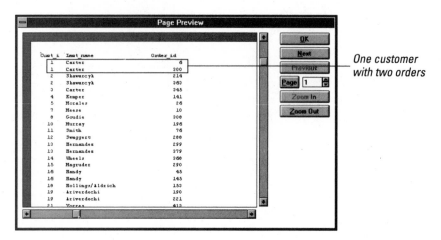

*One customer
with two orders*

This report reflects data from the CUSTOMER table (Cust_id and Last_name) and the ORDERS table (Order_id). Notice that for every customer ID in the CUSTOMER file, there can be many order records in the ORDERS file. The data in this report now reflects the multiple order records for Rita Carter, Cust_id 1, in the ORDERS table.

2   Click the OK push button to close the Page Preview window.

Displaying Fields in Multiple Tables

As indicated earlier, an important feature of relating tables in a View window is that you can display and modify information found in both tables. So that you can look up customer IDs for the contest winner in one table and enter order information for the free gift boxes in the other table, you need to have fields from both tables displayed in the Browse window.

Using the Browse Fields Command

To see the fields you want in the Browse window, you need to use the Browse Fields command in the Command window. After you enter the command, you type the names of the fields you want displayed in the Browse window.

Use the Browse Fields command

Before you begin, be sure Work Area 1 is selected.

1   Click the Command window to make it active.

2   In the first blank line of the Command window, type:

BROWSE FIELDS Cust_id, Last_name, Orders.Order_id, Orders.Order_date, Orders.Gift

---

Tip   If you make a typing error as you enter field names, simply move the insertion point to the location in the line you want to correct, and type over or delete to correct your errors. After you press ENTER, if you get the message "Variable *xyz* not found," it means that you have entered a field name not in the tables. This is probably the result of a typing error. Return to the Command window, correct the line, and then press ENTER. (You do not need to go to the end of the line before you press ENTER.)

You must fully qualify the field names for each field in a table that is not in the selected work area; in other words, you must fully qualify the field names from the ORDERS table. You do not need to fully qualify the field names from the CUSTOMER table, because this table is in the selected work area.

Caution   Modifying the fields that relate the tables can destroy links between the tables. To prevent any changes to these fields, you should avoid displaying them in the Browse window. In this example, Cust_id and Orders.Order_id are included in this exercise only to help you better visualize the relationship of the records in the tables.

---

3   Press ENTER.

The Browse window looks like the following illustration.

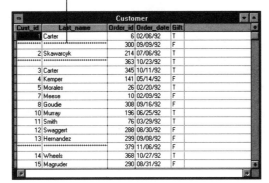

Duplicate data for this customer

The fields containing asterisks represent duplicate data for the record above the field.

Locate fields in the Browse window

With information from both tables available in one Browse window, you can modify order information. First, use the Locate option to find the order record for the winning customer.

1   From the Record menu, choose Locate.

2   Click the For box to display the Expression Builder dialog.

3   From the Fields list, double-click Last_name.

The insertion point appears after the field name in the Locate Record For box.

4   Type = **"Hawthorne"**

5   Click the OK push button.

6   Click the Locate push button.

The record for this customer appears in the Browse window.

Modify fields in the Browse window

Now you can update this customer's order information to show that the second order for this customer is a free gift. Indicate this is a free gift by entering "**T**" (True).

1   Press the down arrow to move to this customer's second order.

2   Press TAB until the Gift field is selected.

3   Type **T**

4   Double-click the Control-menu box in the Browse window.

Establishing Relationships with Additional Tables

As you modify order information, you realize that the specific items requested in an individual order are stored in yet another table; this table is called ORDER.DBF. To complete the changes to the order information, you need to open this table in another work area.

Open another table

1   In the View window, select Work Area 3.

2   In the View window, click the Open push button.

The Open dialog appears.

3   In the Select A Table list, select ORDER.DBF.

4   Click the Open push button.

Open another table

To learn the full name of the box of chocolates, open BOXES.DBF in another work area.

1 In the View window, select Work Area 4.

2 Click the Open push button.

The Open dialog appears.

3 In the Select A Table list, select BOXES.DBF.

4 Click the Open push button.

Now four tables are open: CUSTOMER in Work Area 1, ORDERS in Work Area 2, ORDER in Work Area 3, and BOXES in Work Area 4.

Open the Setup dialog for a table

1 In the View window, select ORDER in Work Area 3.

2 In the View window, click the Setup push button.

The Setup dialog appears.

Create an index file for a child table

The ORDER table does not have an index file associated with it. So that you can relate the ORDERS table to ORDER table, you need to create an index file.

1 In the Indexes area, click the Add push button.

The Open dialog appears.

2 Click the New push button.

The Index dialog appears.

Create an index key

Because you will relate the ORDERS and ORDER tables through the order ID, you need to index the ORDER table on the Order_id field.

1 In the Fields list, be sure Order_id is selected.

2 Click the Add To Index List push button.

The Order_id field appears in the Index Key list. This index key orders the table records by order ID.

3 Click the OK push button to return to the Setup dialog.

Be sure a small key appears next to the tag name "Order: Order_id" in the Indexes list.

4 Click the OK push button to return to the View window.

Open the Setup dialog for another table

1   In the View window, select Work Area 4.

2   Click the Setup push button.

The Setup dialog appears.

Create an index file for another child table

The BOXES table does not have an index file associated with it. So that you can relate the ORDER table to the BOXES table, you need to create an index file.

1   In the Indexes area, click the Add push button.

The Open dialog appears.

2   Click the New push button.

The Index dialog appears.

Create an index key

Because you will relate the ORDER and BOXES tables with the box ID, you need to index the BOXES table on the Box_id field.

1   In the Fields list, select Box_id.

2   Click the Add To Index List push button.

The Box_id field appears in the Index Key list. This index key orders the table records by box ID.

3   Click the OK push button to return to the Setup dialog.

Be sure a small key appears next to the tag name "Boxes: Box_id" in the Indexes list.

4   Click the OK push button to return to the View window.

The arrow next to each table indicates that a sort order is set.

Establish table relationships

Now that the ORDER and BOXES tables have been indexed properly, you can establish the relationships between all the tables.

1   In the View window, select ORDERS in Work Area 2.

2   Click the Relations push button.

3   Select ORDER in Work Area 3.

The Expression Builder dialog appears containing the field name that will relate these tables.

4   Click the OK push button.

ORDERS and ORDER are related by the Order_id field.

5 Select Order in Work Area 3.

6 Click the Relations push button.

7 Select Boxes in Work Area 4.

The Expression Builder dialog appears.

8 Click the OK push button.

ORDER and BOXES are related by the Box_id field.

The View window looks like the following illustration.

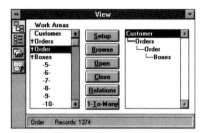

Establish One-to-Many relationships

1 In the View window, select Work Area 1.

2 Click the 1-To-Many push button.

The 1-To-Many dialog appears.

3 In the Child Aliases list, click All.

4 Click the OK push button.

Using Command Window Shortcuts

To see fields from the tables that are not in the currently selected work area, you need to use the Browse Fields command in the Command window. Because you still want to display the fields already specified with the earlier Browse Fields command, as well as the Box_id, Quantity, and Box_name fields, you need to enter these field names (and the name of the table in which the field is located) as part of the Browse Fields command.

To save time and prevent typing errors, you can simply scroll through the Command window until you see the Browse Fields command line you entered earlier in the lesson. With the insertion point at the end of the line, you simply type the additional field names you want included in the Browse window.

Modify the Browse Fields command line

1   From the <u>W</u>indow menu, choose Co<u>mm</u>and.

2   In the Command window, scroll to the command line that looks like the one in the following illustration.

Scroll to this line.

3   With the insertion point anywhere in the command line, press END.

4   At the end of the command line, type:

,Orders.Gift_mess, Order.Quantity, Boxes.Box_name

Because these additional fields are located in child tables, not in the current work area, you need to fully qualify the field names. Be sure to include a comma at the end of the previous line before you type the new fields.

Tip   Anytime you want to repeat a command you entered in the Command window, you can scroll to the command you want and, with the insertion point anywhere in the command line, press ENTER to perform the command again.

---

5   Press ENTER.

The Browse window looks like the following illustration.

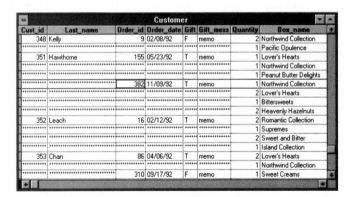

Modify fields in the Browse window

Now you can update the winning customer's order information to include a message that this customer should receive two free boxes.

1   With the record for Hawthorne's order ID 382 still selected, press TAB until the Gift_mess field for the first item is selected.

2   Double-click the word "memo."

The memo editing window opens.

3   Type the following:

Congratulations! You won the Chocolate Lovers of the Month recipe contest. Enjoy these free boxes with our compliments.

4   Close the memo editing window.

5   Press TAB to select the Quantity field.

6   Type **3**

7   Press ENTER

The last order record for this customer now contains two more boxes of the Northwind Collection.

8   Double-click the Control-menu box in the Browse window.

One Step Further

You can save all the relationships, as well as any other settings you have made from the View window in a view file. The next time you want to work with these tables, related in this way, you simply open the view file.

Save your current view file environment

1   Click anywhere in the View window to make it active.

2   From the File menu, choose Save As.

3   In the Save View As box, type **SWEET08**

4   Click the Save push button.

5   Close the View window.

Open another file environment

1   From the File menu, choose Open.

2   In the List Files Of Type popup, select View.

3   In the File Name list, double-click OSFV08.VUE.

4   From the Window menu, choose View.

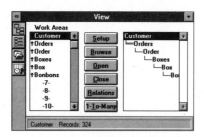

The View window appears in which all the tables for Sweet Lil's are related. Because these relationships are saved in a view file, you can have these relationships (and subsequently all the table information) available without having to open and establish relationships for each individual table.

View a report of related information

To see the breadth of information available to you when you use related tables, generate a report using the report form called OSFR08.FRX.

1 From the Database menu, choose Report.

2 Click the Form push button.

3 Double-click PRACTICE in the Directory list.

4 In the Report File box, double-click OSFR08.FRX.

5 Click the OK push button.

The report appears in the Page Preview window.

6 Click the text on the page to see a closeup view of the report.

7 Click the OK push button to close the Page Preview window.

If You Want to Continue to the Next Lesson

1 From the Window menu, choose Command.

2 In the Command window, type **close all**

3 Press ENTER.

The Close All command closes all windows and files which are open in all work areas.

If You Want to Quit FoxPro for Windows for Now

▶ From the File menu, choose Exit.

Lesson Summary

To	Do this
Relate files in the View window (one-to-one)	From the Window menu, choose View. Open the tables you want to relate. In the Work Areas list, select the parent table. Click the Relations push button. In the Work Areas list, select the child table. Click the OK push button in the Expression Builder dialog to return to the View window.
Relate files in the View window (one-to-many)	First establish a one-to-one relationship. In the View window, select the file in the first work area. Click the 1-To-Many push button. In the 1-To-Many dialog, select the child table from the Child Aliases list. Click the Move push button. Click the OK push button.
Display fields from different files in the Browse window	In the Command window, type the Browse Fields command followed by the list of field names you want displayed. Press ENTER. Use fully-qualified field names for any fields not in the selected work area.
Repeat a Command window command	Scroll to the command you want, and, with the insertion point anywhere in the command line, press ENTER to perform the command again. You can also edit the command line.

For more information on	See in the *Microsoft FoxPro for Windows User's Guide*
Setting relations in the View window	Chapter 7, Window Menu (View)

For more information on	See in the *Microsoft FoxPro for Windows Language Reference*
Browse Fields command	Browse Fields

Preview of the Next Lesson

The lessons in Part 3 of this book introduce you to the FoxPro for Windows power tools. Using tools like the Screen Builder, the Menu Builder, and Application Generator (also known as FoxApp), you will learn how to create customized applications with very little programming. You will see how to create your own menus, windows, and dialogs so that it is even easier to get the information you need.

Review & Practice

The lessons in this part of the book show you how easy it is to manipulate and manage information in your table, whether you work with one file or many. The Review & Practice activity that follows will help you prepare for the lessons in the next part of the book. This is a less structured scenario in which you can practice and refine your file management and reporting skills on your own. Follow the general guidelines—the rest is up to you.

Part 2   Review & Practice

Before you create a table of your own, practice the skills you learned in Part 2 by working through some database management activities. You will start by creating two tables. Then you will relate these tables and the EMPLOYEE table (from Part 1, Review & Practice) in a query. A report you create will show information found in several files. You will also order your data and finally relate tables in the View window so that you can update information in several tables at once.

Scenario

As the PC support manager at Sweet Lil's, you not only help other departments manage their information, but you also keep track of how employees use their personal computers at Sweet Lil's. In this Review & Practice section, you create and use tables that contain personal computing inventory information to improve your own effectiveness. Follow the general guidelines provided in each step. If you need help, use the table at the end of each step for references to additional information in the lessons.

You will review and practice how to:

- Create tables.
- Establish table relationships in a query.
- Use advanced reporting techniques.
- Index a table.
- Establish table relationships in a View window.

Estimated lesson time: 45 minutes

Step 1:   Create Tables

Create a table structure for an equipment table. This table identifies all the personal computing products (hardware and software) used at Sweet Lil's. To help you track how personal computers are being used at Sweet Lil's, you prepared and distributed a personal computing inventory survey. Before the responses are returned, you can create a table structure in which you will enter survey responses.

Create the equipment table structure

This structure contains only two fields: one for the equipment ID and another for the product name that the ID number represents.

Your equipment table structure should look like the following.

Field name in table	Field type	Field length
Equip_id	Numeric	3
Equip_name	Character	40

▶ Save the equipment table with the name **REVT01.DBF**

Create the inventory table structure

Create a structure based on the survey form in the following illustration.

PERSONAL COMPUTER SURVEY

Name: _____

Employee ID: _____

List the personal computer hardware and software you use:

Product Name   Date Purchased   Depreciated? (Y/N)

1 You can use whatever field names and field lengths you wish, but here are some guidelines:

Name on form	Field name in table	Field type	Field length
Product Name	Equip_id	Numeric	3
Employee ID	Empl_id	Numeric	3
Date Purchased	Purchased	Date	-
Depreciated?	Depreciatd	Logical	1

Note   Even though the users supply the name of the product, you will use the Equip_id field from the table you created in the previous step.

2 Save the inventory table with the name **REVT02.DBF**

Both tables seem small enough to be combined in a single file. However, such a table would become unnecessarily large, because it would contain a lot of repeated data. For example, for every employee that uses a word processing application, there would be a field that contained the name of the application. Repeated over dozens of employees (and many more as Sweet Lil's expands and adds staff) such information could require a great deal of valuable disk space. By separating the information in two tables, you use disk space more efficiently. With an Equip_id field in both tables, you can relate these tables and get information from both of them at the same time.

For more information on	See
Defining a New Table Structure	Lesson 5
Specifying Fields	Lesson 5

Step 2:   Establish Table Relationships in a Query

With the help of an intern, all the responses to your inventory survey are entered in a table called INVENTRY; this table has the same structure as your REVT02 table. Your intern also entered personal computer hardware and software information in a table called EQUIPMNT; this table has the same structure as the REVT01 table. So that you can see how individual employees use their personal computer, open the tables that contain this data.

Create a query to join the INVENTRY and EQUIPMNT tables

1   Use the New option on the File menu to create new file. Then specify that you want to create a query. When you see the Open dialog, be sure the REVIEW directory is open, and then double-click INVENTRY in the Select A Table list.

2   In the RQBE window, click the Add push button in the Tables area. When you see the Open dialog, double-click EQUIPMNT in the Select A Table list. Click the OK push button in the RQBE Join Condition dialog, which displays the common field (Equip_id) by which these tables are related.

3   Click the Fields check box to select the Equip_name field from the EQUIPMNT table so that this field appears in the list of output fields.

4   Drag the Mover button for the Equip_name field to just below the Equip_id field.

Save a query

▶   From the File menu, choose Save. In the Directory popup, be sure \PRACTICE\REVIEW is the current directory. Save your query with the name **REVQ02.QPR**

Do the query and close the Browse window

1   Click the Do Query push button, and examine the hardware and software information for each employee.

2   Close the query window when you are finished.

Join another file in the query

So that you can see the employee's last name, add the EMPLOYEE table to the query relationship.

1   In the RQBE window, click the Add push button in the Tables area. When you see the Open dialog, double-click EMPLOYEE in the Select A Table list. Click the OK push button in the RQBE Join Condition dialog, which displays the common field (Empl_id) by which these tables are related.

2   Click the Fields check box to select the Last_name fields from the EMPLOYEE table so that this field appears in the list of output fields. Click the OK push button to return to the RQBE window.

3   Save the query.

Do the query and close the Browse window

1   Click the Do Query push button, and examine the hardware and software information for each employee.

2   Close the query window when you are finished.

For more information on	See
Connecting Multiple Tables	Lesson 6
Joining Tables	Lesson 6

Step 3:   Use Advanced Reporting Techniques

The new vice president of Operations wants to see a report of computer use by department. After you revise the query to include the Department field as one of the output fields, direct the query results to a report form you create.

Modify the query

1   Click the Fields check box to select the Department field from the EMPLOYEE table so that this field appears in the list of output fields. Because you are displaying the full product name of the equipment, you do not need to display the Equip_id field. Similarly, because you are displaying the employee last name, you do not need the Empl_id field. Remove these fields from the Output Fields list, and then return to the RQBE window.

2   With the RQBE window for your query still open, select Report/Label from the Output popup.

Create a report

1   Click the Options check box to see the RQBE Display Options dialog. Choose the Report radio button, and then click the Quick Report check box. In the RQBE Quick Report dialog, choose the large button on the left to display records in a format of rows and columns. Click the OK push button twice to return to the RQBE window.

2   Save your changes to the query.

3   Do the Query to display the report in the Page Preview window.

4 Click anywhere in the display area to get a close-up view of the report. Click the OK push button to return to the RQBE window. Minimize the RQBE window.

Modify the report form

Your report is not quite ready to present to the vice president. Organize the information on the report so that it looks like the following illustration when you are done.

```
                                    Computer Use By Department


       Dept #   Product Name                      Date          Depreciated ?      Employee
                                                Purchased

       EXEC     Microsoft Word for Windows 2.0    05/12/92            Y            Hamilton
       EXEC     Microsoft Excel for Windows 4.0   05/12/92            Y            Hamilton
       EXEC     Microsoft Project for Windows 3.0 09/16/92            Y            Hamilton
       EXEC     Microsoft Access for Windows 1.0  12/02/92            Y            Hamilton
       EXEC     Microsoft Word for Windows 2.0    10/14/92            Y            Stewart
       EXEC     Microsoft Excel for Windows 4.0   10/14/92            Y            Stewart
       EXEC     Microsoft Project for Windows 3.0 10/14/92            Y            Stewart
       EXEC     Microsoft Word for Windows 2.0    10/14/92            Y            Anderson
                  8         Applications

       INFO     Microsoft Word for Windows 2.0    10/14/92            Y            Fallon
       INFO     Microsoft Excel for Windows 4.0   10/14/92            Y            Fallon
       INFO     Microsoft Project for Windows 3.0 10/14/92            Y            Fallon
       INFO     Microsoft Access for Windows 1.0  12/02/92            Y            Fallon
       INFO     Microsoft Word for Windows 2.0    11/18/92            Y            Danielson
       INFO     Microsoft Excel for Windows 4.0   11/18/92            Y            Danielson
       INFO     Microsoft Access for Windows 1.0  12/02/92            Y            Danielson
                  7         Applications

       MANU     Microsoft Word for Windows 2.0    10/14/92            Y            Fortis
       MANU     Microsoft Project for Windows 3.0 10/14/92            Y            Fortis
       MANU     Microsoft Project for Windows 3.0 10/14/92            Y            Robert
       MANU     Microsoft Excel for Windows 4.0   10/14/92            Y            Williams
       MANU     Microsoft Access for Windows 1.0  12/02/92            Y            Williams
       MANU     Microsoft Excel for Windows 4.0   10/14/92            Y            Chu
       MANU     Microsoft Project for Windows 3.0 10/14/92            Y            Chu
       MANU     Microsoft Word for Windows 2.0    10/14/92            Y            Chu
       MANU     Microsoft Access for Windows 1.0  12/02/92            Y            McIntyre
                  9         Applications

       MRKT     Microsoft Word for Windows 2.0    10/14/92            Y            Hamilton
       MRKT     Microsoft Project for Windows 3.0 10/14/92            Y            Hamilton
       MRKT     Microsoft Word for Windows 2.0    10/14/92            Y            Oshefski
                  3         Applications

       OPER     Microsoft Excel for Windows 4.0   10/14/92            Y            Hamilton
       OPER     Microsoft Project for Windows 3.0 10/14/92            Y            Hamilton
       OPER     Microsoft Word for Windows 2.0    10/14/92            Y            Calvin
       OPER     Microsoft Word for Windows 2.0    10/14/92            Y            Buckley
                  4         Applications

       01/17/93
```

1 From the File menu, choose Open. After you verify the REVIEW directory is open, select Report from the List Files Of Type popup. Then double-click the report file called REVQ02.FRX.

2 Select all the objects in the Page Header band, and delete them.

Text tool

3 Use the text tool to place a report title centered near the top of the Report Layout window. Near the top of the Report Layout window, use the text tool to create the report title, **Computer Use By Department.**

4 Drag the sizing box for the Page Header bar downward about one inch.

5 Change the page orientation by choosing Page Layout from the Report menu. Then click the Print Setup push button. In the Orientation area, click the Landscape radio button. Click the OK push button until you return to the Report Layout window.

Arrange the columns

1 Drag the field objects so that they appear in the following order:

Department
Equip_name
Purchased
Depreciatd
Last_name

2 Arrange the fields so that they are spaced evenly and they span the width of the page, so that the right edge of the Last_name field is at the 8-inch mark.

Enter new column headings

1 Use the text tool to type the following column titles:

Use this heading	For this field
Dept #	Department
Product Name	Equip_name
Date Purchased	Purchased
Depreciated ?	Depreciatd
Employee	Last_name

Tip You can place the "Date Purchased" column title on two lines.

2 To make your report easier to read, make the column titles bold.

Group data in a report

The vice president wants to see a report of application software used in each department. Group your report data by department.

▶ Group the report data by department, using the Data Grouping option on the Report menu. In the Group Info dialog, click the Group push button to display the Expression Builder dialog. Select the EMPLOYEE table, and then double-click Department from the Fields list. Click the OK push button until you return to the Group Info dialog. Clear the New Page check box. Click the OK push button to return to the Report Layout window.

Create a band of data and a calculated field

The vice president wants to see the total number of applications used in each department. You need to a create a total field for each data group.

1 Drag the Sizing box for the Group Footer bar downward to the ¼-inch mark.

2 Select the field tool, and create a field in the Group Footer band. Place it under the Equip_name field. In the Report Expression dialog, click the Calculate check box. In the Calculate dialog, click the Count radio button. (This selection counts the number of records in this group.) Click the OK push button to return to the Report Expression dialog. Click the Expression push button. In the Expression Builder dialog, select the table for the Equip_id field. Click the OK push button in each dialog until you return to the Report Layout window.

3 Use the line tool to draw a line in the Group Footer band to separate the detail records from the Group Footer band.

4 Use the text tool to create a label to the right of the new field. Type **Applications**

5 Close the Report window, and then click the Yes push button when you are asked whether you want to save changes to the report form.

Modify the query

Because the vice president wants to see a report of application software used in each department, add another selection criterion to display records in which the Equip_id is greater than 600, but less than 700. (In the EQUIPMNT table, you assigned application software IDs starting at 601 and ending at 699.)

1 Restore the RQBE window by double-clicking the RQBE icon at the bottom of your window.

2 Click the Order By check box, and then order the records by the department field. You can sort within each department by last name. Click the OK push button to return to the RQBE window.

3 In the Selection Criteria area, add a selection criterion to display records that have an equipment ID between 600 and 700 in the EQUIPMNT table.

Hint Use Between as the comparison operator. Type 600, 700 in the Example column.

---

4 Do the query to view your report. Close all your open files and windows. Click the Yes push button when you see the message asking whether you want to save changes to the query.

For more information on	See
Creating a Band of Data	Lesson 6
Grouping Data in a Report	Lesson 6
Creating a Computed Field	Lesson 6

Step 4:   Index Tables

So that you can order records in each table efficiently, use the Setup dialog for each table to add index keys.

1   Use the View window to open each table in separate work areas, according to the following table.

In this work area	Open this file
1	INVENTRY
2	EMPLOYEE
3	EQUIPMNT

2   Click the Setup push button after you select the file in each work area. Create new CDX files with the following index keys, and set the sort order indicated with the sort key.

Table	Index key on
Inventry	Empl_id (sort key)
	Equip_id
	Purchased
Employee	Empl_id (sort key)
	Last_name
	Hire_date
Equipmnt	Equip_id (sort key)

Tip   Use the Indexes area of the Setup dialog.

For more information on	See
Understanding Indexing	Lesson 7
Adding an Index Key	Lesson 7

Step 5: Establish Table Relationships in a View Window

Relating files in a View window allows you to modify the records displayed in the Browse window, while relating files in a query does not. Use the View window to relate all the files currently open. When you are done, your View window will look like the following illustration.

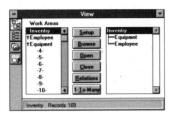

Sweet Lil's has just purchased Microsoft FoxPro for Windows for the Human Resources staff. So that you can add additional records reflecting the purchases of this software, establish relationships for these files in the View window.

1 In the View window, select INVENTRY in Work Area 1. Click the Relations push button. Click EMPLOYEE in Work Area 2. The Expression Builder dialog suggests that Work Area 1 and Work Area 2 can be related by the Empl_id field. Click the OK push button to return to the View window.

2 With Work Area 1 still selected, click the Relations push button. Click EQUIPMNT in Work Area 3. The Expression Builder dialog suggests that Work Area 1 and Work Area 3 can be related by the Equip_id field. Click the OK push button to return to the View window.

3 With Work Area 1 still selected, click the 1-To-Many push button. In the 1-To-Many dialog, click the All push button, and then click the OK push button to establish one-to-many relationships between INVENTRY and the other files.

4 Use the Browse Fields command in the Command window to display these fields:

Employee.department, Equip_id, Equipmnt.equip_name, Purchased, Depreciatd, Empl_id, Employee.last_name, Employee.comments

With the INVENTRY file as the current table, you need to include the table name for the fields from the other tables.

Update the tables

Now you can update your database information.

1 You need to add a new record to the EQUIPMNT table in its own Browse window. In the View window, double-click EQUIPMNT to open its Browse window. From the Browse menu, choose Append Record.

- In the Equip_id field, type **605**

- In the Equip_name field, type **Microsoft FoxPro for Windows, 2.5**

2 Close the EQUIPMNT Browse window.

3 Be sure INVENTRY is still selected in the View window.

4 In the Browse window for the fields in the related files (you can locate the Browse Fields command in the Command window, and then press ENTER to redisplay the Browse window), add a new record for both people on the Human Resources staff.

From the Browse menu, choose Append Record. For employee ID 22 and employee ID 24, enter the following information:

- Indicate they purchased the equipment ID 605 on 6/1/93.

- This product is already depreciated.

- Enter a note in the Comment field indicating that they are scheduled to attend product training on 6/8/93.

For more information on	See
Establishing Relationships in the View Window	Lesson 8
Relating Tables One-to-One	Lesson 8
Relating Tables One-to-Many	Lesson 8
Displaying Fields in Multiple Tables	Lesson 8

If You Want to Continue to the Next Lesson

1 From the Window menu, choose Command.

2 In the Command window, type **close all**

3 Press ENTER.

The Close All command closes all windows and files which are open in all work areas.

4 Double-click the Control-menu box in the View window.

If You Want to Quit FoxPro for Windows for Now

▶ From the File menu, choose Exit.

3 Creating Your Own Applications

Creating Custom Screens

You can design and build your own applications with the powerful capability provided in FoxPro for Windows. By creating applications that meet your specific information requirements, other people in your company can use database information without learning FoxPro for Windows commands.

Your first step in creating your own applications is to create custom screens. In this lesson, you will learn how to use Quick Screen to generate a simple input and editing window. You will use the Screen Design window to customize fields and field titles and to create graphic screen objects. After you generate screen code, you will run your custom screen. Then you will modify an existing screen by adding popups and other controls, such as push buttons and spinner controls.

In the remaining lessons in this book, you will switch back and forth from being an application developer to being an application user. When you see information regarding "the user" it refers to the hypothetical user for whom you are creating an application.

You will learn how to:

- Create a Quick Screen.
- Place fields in a screen.
- Create push buttons.
- Enter code snippets.
- Generate screen code.
- Handle errors.
- Create popups.
- Create a spinner control.

Estimated lesson time: 50 minutes

If you closed FoxPro for Windows at the end of the last lesson

▶ Start FoxPro for Windows by double-clicking the FoxPro for Windows icon.

Using the Screen Builder

You are not limited to using the Browse or Change window to view and enter table information. Although these windows are adequate for most purposes, they have their limitations. For example, the 10-character limit for a field title is often a rather cryptic indication of what the user should enter in a field. In other situations, you might want to minimize errors by restricting the user from making an entry in a field.

With the Screen Builder in FoxPro for Windows, you can create custom screens that make it easier to enter and maintain database information. A screen that is easy to read and use ensures proper and efficient use of your database system.

The Screen Builder includes two tools you can use to create your own custom screens: Quick Screen and the Screen Design window. Quick Screen generates a basic screen that automatically contains the fields and field titles found in the current table. In the Screen Design window, you can modify the screen to give your custom screen the same appearance and features you see in other Microsoft Windows applications. The toolbox in the Screen Design window contains the tools you use to create and modify the following:

- **Graphic objects**, such as lines and boxes.
- **Screen control objects**, such as push buttons, popups, radio buttons, check boxes, and lists.
- **Field characteristics**, such as restricting input to a field.

Note FoxPro for Windows uses the word *screen* when you are working in the Screen Design window. The word *window* refers to the screen when the user runs it as a screen program.

Open a table

To create a screen in which you can display and modify Sweet Lil's bonbon information, open the BONBONS table.

1 From the Window menu, choose View.

2 In the View window, click the Open push button.

3 In the Directory list, double-click PRACTICE to make it the current directory.

PRACTICE is already the current directory if you did not exit FoxPro for Windows at the end of the last lesson.

4 In the Select A Table list, select BONBONS.DBF.

5 Click the Open push button.

Set the table order

So that the records appear in bonbon ID order, you need to set the sort order in the Setup dialog.

1 In the View window, click the Setup push button.

2 In the Indexes area, be sure the Bonbons:Bonbon_id tag is selected.

3 Click the Set Order push button.

This ensures that the records are displayed alphabetically by bonbon ID.

4 Click the OK push button to return to the View window.

Create a new screen file

1 From the File menu, choose New.

The New dialog appears.

2 Click the Screen radio button.

3 Click the New push button.

The Screen Design window appears.

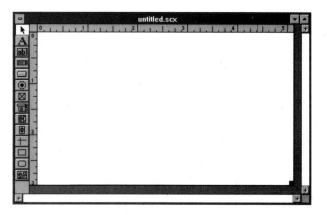

Using Quick Screen

Quick Screen is a fast way to create a screen based on the fields in the current table.

1 From the Screen menu, choose Quick Screen.

The Quick Screen dialog appears.

2   In the Field Layout area, click the large push button on the right.

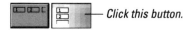 — *Click this button.*

This selection displays the fields and field titles in rows in a layout similar to what you see in the Change window. Verify that the Titles and Add Alias check boxes are checked and that the Fields and Memory Variables check boxes are cleared.

3   Click the OK push button.

Using the Screen Design Window

Now that you have created a basic screen, you can use the tools in the Screen Design window toolbox to customize the screen. These tools allow you to be as creative as you wish when you lay out fields, titles, graphic objects, and controls. In the interest of good design principles, this lesson focuses on using many, but not all, of the tools in the toolbox.

The Screen Design window toolbox looks like the following illustration.

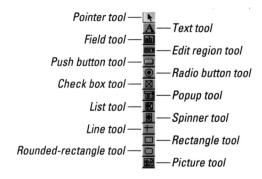

Adjust the screen size

To give yourself enough space to work in, enlarge the screen.

▶   Drag the lower-right corner of the screen until the screen is about 3½ inches long and 5 inches wide.

Display ruler lines

Ruler lines make it easier to lay out objects on the screen.

1   From the Screen menu, choose Ruler/Grid.

The Ruler/Grid dialog appears.

2   In the Ruler Lines area, click the Yes radio button.

3 Click the OK push button.

Ruler lines appear in the Screen Design window.

Move field objects in a window

In the same way that you use click and drag techniques to select and move objects in the Report Layout window, you can select and move objects in the Screen Design window. Use the following illustration as a guide for the design of your new screen.

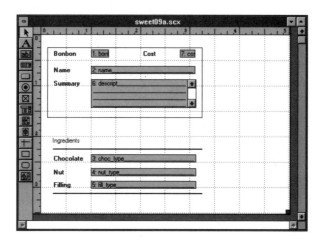

Tip To place objects on the screen more precisely, you can turn off Snap To Grid. Or, with Snap To Grid still on, you can use the arrow keys to move selected objects one pixel at a time.

You can SHIFT+CLICK to select multiple screen objects.

You can drag a selection marquee around all the objects located at the left edge, by dragging from the center of the screen to the left edge.

1 Select the Cost field and its field title.

2 Drag the objects so that the Cost field is at the top edge of the window and its right edge is even with the right edge of the Name field below it.

3 Select the Choc_type, Nut_type, and Fill_type fields and their field titles.

4 Drag the selected objects downward to the bottom third of the screen.

5 Adjust the size of the Descript field so that it is as wide as the Name field and about ½-inch high.

6 Adjust the size of the Choc_type, Nut_type, and Fill_type fields so that they are as wide as the Name field.

7 Select the Descript field and title.

8 Drag the objects to just under the Name field.

9 Select all of the objects in the top half of the screen.

10   Arrange all the objects so that there is about one line of space separating each object on the screen.

11   Drag the objects so that they are positioned as shown in the preceding illustration.

Save the screen file

To store the work you have completed so far, save your screen file.

Tip   As you work in the Screen Design window, be sure to save your changes frequently.

---

1   From the File menu, choose Save As.

The Save As dialog appears.

2   In the Save Screen As box, type **SWEET09A**

3   Click the Save push button.

4   Click the Yes push button when you see the message asking whether you want to save the environment.

The environment you are saving with the screen file includes the table and its current sort order. When the user runs this screen, the screen program will automatically open the table with the sort order already set. This not only saves time but also ensures that the user will use the correct table.

Draw lines and boxes

Box tool

Line tool

1   Click the rectangle tool.

2   Draw a box that surrounds all the objects in the top part of the window.

3   Click the line tool.

4   Draw a line just above the Choc_type field.

5   From the Object menu, choose Pen.

6   In the cascading menu, select 2 Point.

7   With the line still selected, from the Edit menu, choose Copy.

8   From the Edit menu, choose Paste.

9   Drag the line down to just below the Fill_type field, and align it with the line above.

Your screen looks like the following illustration.

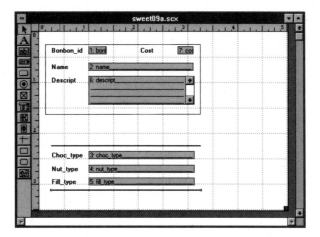

10 From the File menu, choose Save to store the work you have completed so far.

Change field titles

Give the field titles more descriptive names to more easily identify them.

1 Double-click the text tool.

2 Drag the pointer across the Bonbon_id field title to select it.

3 Type **Bonbon**

4 Repeat steps 2 and 3 to change each of the following field titles according to this table.

Current title	New title
Descript	Summary
Choc_type	Chocolate
Nut_type	Nut
Fill_type	Filling

5 At the left edge of the screen, click about 2 inches from the top, and then type **Ingredients**

6 From the File menu, choose Save to store the work you have completed so far.

Your screen looks like the following illustration.

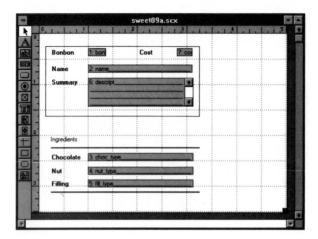

Naming the Screen

The Screen Layout dialog allows you to select a number of options for your screen. You can give your custom screen a title that appears in the title bar at the top of the screen. You can also specify the kind of window, colors and fonts, and the environment (tables, sort order, and any relationships). For this screen, you will center the screen and give it a title.

Give the screen a title and a name

1   From the Screen menu, choose Layout.

The Screen Layout dialog appears.

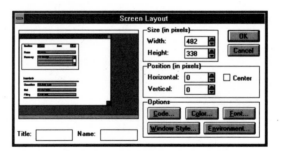

2   In the Title box, type **Sweet Lil's Bonbons**

As the words you type fill the box, the text scrolls to the left to give you more room for your entry.

3   In the Name box, type **Bonbons**

This allows screen code to refer to the screen by this name, rather than by the more cryptic default name. Using a name you provide makes screen code easier to read.

4   In the Position area, click the Center check box.

The Screen Layout dialog looks like the following illustration.

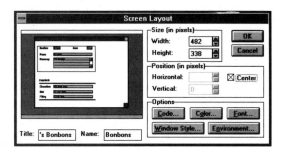

Setting Window Attributes

From the Screen Layout dialog, you can also specify the attributes you want in your window. For example, your window can have the ability to be minimized, to be moved, to be closed, or to have a title bar that is half the usual height. You can also specify the kind of border to surround your window.

1   In the Options area, click the Window Style push button.

The Window Style dialog appears.

2   In the Attributes area, click the Close check box.

This gives the user the ability to close the window by using the Control-menu box.

3   Click the OK push button to return to the Screen Layout dialog.

4   Click the OK push button to return to the Screen Design window.

Modifying Field Attributes

The Bonbon_id field on your custom screen allows you to change the bonbon ID for a specific bonbon record. Because of the relationships between the BONBONS table and the other tables, you must be very careful not to delete or change the Bonbon_id field. Doing so could destroy the ability to relate the BONBONS table to other tables. To prevent the user from making destructive changes, you can make this field a display-only field.

Make a display-only field

1 In the Screen Design window, double-click the Bonbon_id field.

The Field dialog appears.

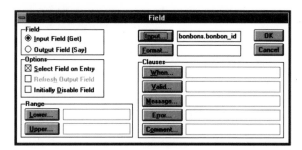

2 In the Field area, click the Output Field (Say) radio button.

This changes the Bonbon_id field so that it can only display data and not accept input from the user.

3 In the Options area, click the Refresh Output Field check box.

This indicates this field will *refresh* when a new record displays; in other words, this field displays new data when the user moves to a new record in the table.

4 Click the OK push button.

Now the data displayed in this field cannot be changed.

Creating Push Buttons

Your screen now looks great, but it does not actually do anything yet. For example, you want to be able to advance through the next records in the table and also return to previous records. You also want to be able to exit quickly from the window.

In the Screen Design window, you can create push buttons that perform a combination of commands with the click of one button. You can also create other *controls* (such as radio buttons, spinners, check boxes, popups, and lists) to make it easier to use your screen.

Creating controls in a screen requires that you use a variable or a field name to store the results. Like a field, a *memory variable* contains the value of an entry or the result of an action. Unlike a field, its value is temporary and is not stored in the table. When creating push buttons that control the application, specify a memory variable name instead of a field.

When you have completed these steps, your screen will look like the following illustration.

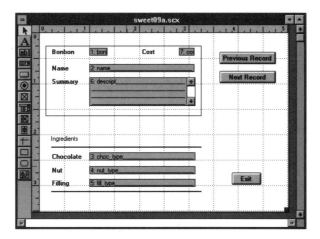

Create a push button

First, create a push button to allow the user to exit quickly from the window.

1   Click in the Screen Design window to make it active.

2   Click the push button tool.

Push button tool

3   Click the push button pointer in an empty area in the lower-right corner of the window.

The Push Button dialog appears.

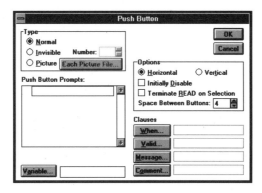

4   In the Push Button Prompts box, type **Exit**

This is the name that will appear on the push button.

5   In the Options area, click the Terminate <u>R</u>EAD On Selection check box.

Checking this box indicates that you want the custom window to close and the screen program to terminate when the user clicks this push button in the window.

6   In the box next to the Variable push button, type **m_exit**

This stores the results of the action to a memory variable called m_exit.

The Push Button dialog looks like the following illustration.

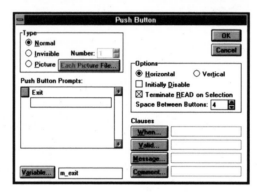

7   Click the OK push button to return to the Screen Design window.

8   From the <u>F</u>ile menu, choose <u>S</u>ave to store the work you have completed so far.

Understanding Code Snippets

A *code snippet* is a set of FoxPro for Windows commands that performs an operation when the user selects a control, such as a push button or check box, in a window. For example, when the user of your custom screen clicks the Next Record push button, you want the next record in the table to be displayed in the custom screen. To do this, you need to provide commands in the form of a code snippet in the Push Button dialog.

Create another push button

1   In the Screen Design window, click the push button tool.

2   Click the pointer in an empty area in the upper-right portion of the window, above the Exit push button you have just created.

The Push Button dialog appears.

3   In the Push Button Prompts box, type **Next Record**

This is the name that will appear on the push button.

Specifying Code Snippets

There are several areas in the Push Button dialog where you can enter code snippets. These areas are known as *clauses*. For example, when you enter a code snippet for a Message clause, you are specifying that a message displays in the status bar when the users move to the control. When you enter a code snippet for a Valid clause, you are specifying what happens when the user clicks the push button.

Enter push button code snippets

Make these changes in the Push Button dialog so that clicking the Next Record push button causes the screen to display data for the next record in the table.

1 Click the Valid push button.

The Code Snippet window appears. In this window, you can enter a code snippet that determines what will happen when the user clicks the push button.

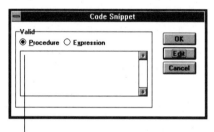

Place insertion point here.

2 In the Code Snippet window, place the insertion point in the text box.

3 Type **skip 1**

This instructs FoxPro for Windows to move to the next record in the table. The number after the Skip command indicates the number of records to skip. For example, if you want to skip through the table five records at a time, enter **skip 5**. To skip one record, you can simply enter **skip** without a number; the Skip command without a number skips one record by default.

4 Press ENTER.

5 On the next line, type **show gets**

The Code Snippet window looks like the following illustration.

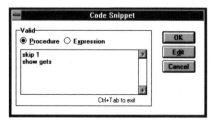

Each of the fields in your custom screen is an *input* field (except the Bonbon_id field). This means that each field needs to get information from the user or from the table. In fact, a command called Get stores information in each field. The Show Gets command displays the information it gets after skipping to the next record in the table. Clearing the fields of previous data and displaying new data is called *refreshing* the fields.

6   Click the OK push button to return to the Push Button dialog.

7   In the box next to the Variable push button, type **m_next**

This stores the results of the action to a memory variable called "m_next."

8   Click the OK push button to return to the Screen Design window.

9   From the File menu, choose Save to store the work you have completed so far.

Create another push button

1   In the Screen Design window, click the push button tool.

Push button tool

2   Click the pointer just above the Next Record push button you have just created.

When you release the push button, the Push Button dialog appears.

3   In the Push Button Prompts box, type **Previous Record**

Enter code snippets

Make these changes in the Push Button dialog so that clicking the Previous Record push button causes the screen to display the previous record in the table.

1   Click the Valid push button.

2   In the Code Snippet window, place the insertion point in the text box.

3   Type **skip -1**

This instructs FoxPro for Windows to move to the previous record in the table.

4   Press ENTER.

5   On the next line of the window, type **show gets**

The Show Gets command displays the information it gets after moving to the previous record in the table.

6   Click the OK push button to return to the Push Button dialog.

7   In the box next to the Variable push button, type **m_prev**

This stores the results of the action to a memory variable called "m_prev."

8   Click the OK push button to return to the Screen Design window.

9   Adjust the size and position of the push buttons so that your screen looks like the following illustration.

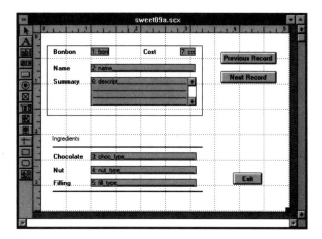

Generating Screen Code

Before you can use your custom screen, you must generate *screen code*. The screen code consists of all the command language instructions, specifications, and layout information about a screen that is executed when you run the screen.

Generate screen code

1   From the Program menu, choose Generate.

2   Click the Yes push button when you see the message asking whether you want to save changes to SWEET09A.SCX.

3   In the Generate Screen dialog, click the Generate push button.

After a moment, the code for your screen is generated and then stored in a file called SWEET09A.SPR.

Running a Screen

Your screen code is actually a FoxPro for Windows program. It is stored in a file with the same name as the screen layout specifications, but the name has the SPR extension. To use a screen, you need to run the screen program.

Run the screen

1   From the Run menu, choose Screen.

The Open dialog appears.

2   In the Screen To Run list, select SWEET09A.SPR.

3   Click the Run push button.

The custom screen you created appears as a window.

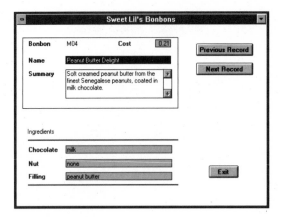

Move to the next record

▶ Click the Next Record push button on your window.

Move to the previous record

▶ Click the Previous Record push button on your window.

Experiment with using the push buttons to move through the table.

Warning   If you press the Previous Record push button when you are at the beginning of the table (or if you press the Next Record push button when you are at the end of the table), you get the error described in the next section. Do not be concerned. Just skip the next step, and continue with the next section.

Cancel the screen program

After scrolling through the table, you can close the window and cancel the screen program.

▶ Click the Exit push button on your window.

Understanding What to Do When Things Go Wrong

Writing code snippets is a simple way to learn how to write programs and use the command language to affect how a screen and its controls will work. But like programming, creating code snippets is often a trial-and-error process of specifying a code snippet, testing the results in a few situations, and then modifying the snippet to adjust for variations you had not anticipated. When you are entering code snippets, it is not uncommon to make a typing mistake or some other error that leads to unexpected results. Programmers often refer to these unexpected results as *bugs*. The process of identifying and correcting bugs is known as *debugging*. In short, finding bugs and debugging are common activities when you are creating code snippets, and it is important to know what to do when bugs happen.

The bug in the Next Record and Previous Record push buttons happened because you did not tell FoxPro for Windows what to do if it could not perform the desired operation. When the first record of the table displays, there is no previous record to skip to. Similarly, when the last record of the table displays, there is no next record to skip to. Subsequently, there is no record data for the Show Gets command to display. For now, you will clear the error message so that you can continue with the following steps in the lesson.

Run the screen

If you did not get an error as you experimented with the push buttons in the previous steps, run the screen again. So that you can learn what to do when an error occurs, click the Previous Record push button to force an error.

1   From the <u>R</u>un menu, choose <u>S</u>creen.

The Open dialog appears.

2   In the Screen To Run list, select SWEET09A.SPR.

3   Click the Run push button.

Move to the previous record

▶   Click the Previous Record push button on your window until this message displays:

Handling Error Messages

When you see the Program Error message box, the three push buttons correspond to the different actions you can take.

Click	To do this	Results
Cancel	Exit from the screen program, and debug the screen code directly in the screen program window.	The Cancel push button clears the message box and displays the screen program window for your screen program. Double-click the Control-menu box to close the window. Then double-click the Control-menu box in the custom screen to close the screen you created. Then you can correct the error.

Click	To do this	Results
Suspend	Examine the screen code directly in the screen program window and then continue.	The Suspend push button temporarily suspends the action of the screen program. Use the command window to examine memory variables, execute other commands, and examine your code. Close the window and continue running the screen from the point at which the error occurred.
Ignore	Continue running the screen program.	The Ignore push button allows you to continue using the screen without correcting the error.

Clear the error message

1 Click the Ignore push button to clear the message box.

2 Click the Exit push button on your custom screen to cancel the screen program.

3 Close the Screen Design window.

Creating Popup Controls

The screen you created uses simple fields to display data. To give your screen a professional look, however, you can use other controls, such as popups, to display and enter data. When you create a popup, you specify a list of selections from which the user can choose. Popups are especially useful when you want to restrict the entries the user can make.

Open another screen file

1 From the File menu, choose Open.

The Open dialog appears.

2 In the List Files Of Type popup, select Screen.

3 In the File Name list, select LSNS09B.

4 Click the Open push button.

The Screen Design window for this screen appears.

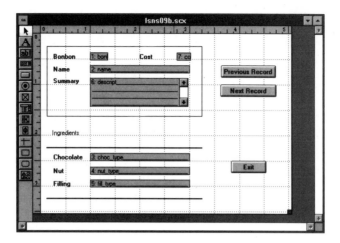

This screen file contains many of the same features found in the screen you created earlier. It also contains code snippets that you can use to minimize the amount of typing you have to do in this lesson. Other code snippets included in this screen file prevent the errors you saw in the previous step. You can learn more about these code snippets in Appendix A, "Clarifying Code Snippets."

Save the screen file with a new name

Before you make any changes to this file, save the file with a new name. By working in a copy of the file, you leave the original file intact so that you can repeat this exercise if you wish.

1 From the File menu, choose Save As.

The Save As dialog appears.

2 In the Save Screen As box, type **SWEET09B**

3 Click the Save push button.

Create a popup control

Use a popup control to display chocolate types from which the user can choose. This popup control replaces the current Choc_type field on your custom screen.

1 In the Screen Design window, select the Choc_type field and press DEL.

Popup tool

2 Click the popup tool in the toolbox.

3 Click near where the Choc_type field was located.

The Popup dialog appears.

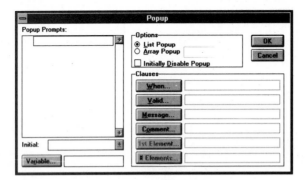

4   In the Popup Prompts list, type **bittersweet**

5   Press the down arrow key to add another item to the list.

6   In the Popup Prompts list, type **dark**

Add the following additional chocolate types to the list. Press the down arrow key after each entry.

fudge
milk
white

7   In the text box next to the Variable push button, type **choc_type**

Specifying this field name ensures that whatever the user selects from this popup will be stored in the Choc_type field in the table. It also ensures that the contents of this field for the current record displays in the window.

The Popup dialog looks like the following illustration.

Indicates items from the Popup Prompts list will be the options that appear in this popup.

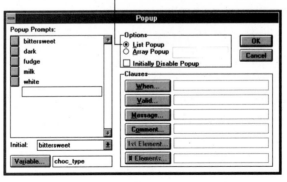

8   Click the OK push button.

9   From the File menu, choose Save to store the work you have completed so far.

Create another popup control

Use a popup control to display nut types from which the user can choose. This popup control replaces the current Nut_type field on your custom screen.

1   In the Screen Design window, select the Nut_type field and press DEL.

2   Click the popup tool in the toolbox.

Popup tool

3   Click near where the Nut_type field was located.

The Popup dialog appears.

Click this radio button to get a list of options from an array.

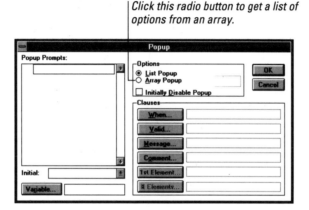

4   In the Options area, click the Array Popup radio button.

5   In the Array Popup box, type **m_nuttypes**

This selection indicates that the popup list will contain items from an array called m_nuttypes. An *array* is a list of data items stored in a special memory variable. Each item is listed in the array so that a program can use an item simply by specifying its location in the array (the first item, the second item, and so on). The array supplying data to this popup is included as a setup code snippet in this screen file.

Important   Using arrays allow you to fill the popup list without typing in each item, which saves you time in completing this exercise. It is also useful when you want to use this same list of items in other screens. Developing your own arrays is an advanced programming technique that is not covered in this book. You can learn more about arrays in the *Microsoft FoxPro for Windows Developer's Guide*.

---

6   In the box next to the Variable push button, type **nut_type**

Specifying this field name ensures that whatever the user selects from this popup will be stored in the Nut_type field in the table. It also ensures that the contents of this field for the current record displays in the window.

7   Click the OK push button.

8   From the File menu, choose Save to store the work you have completed so far.

Create another popup control

Use a popup control to display filling types from which the user can choose. This popup control replaces the current Fill_type field on your custom screen.

1   In the Screen Design window, select the Fill_type field and press DEL.

2   Click the popup tool in the toolbox.

3   Click near where the Fill_type field was located.

The Popup dialog appears.

4   In the Options area, click the Array Popup radio button.

5   In the Array Popup box, type **m_filltypes**

This selection indicates that the popup list will contain items from an array called "m_filltypes." The array supplying data to this popup is included as a setup code snippet in this screen file.

6   In the box next to the Variable, type **fill_type**

Specifying this field name ensures that whatever the user selects from this popup will be stored in the Fill_type field in the table. It also ensures that the contents of this field for the current record displays in the window.

7   Click the OK push button.

8   In the Screen Design window, arrange the new popups so that the screen looks like the following illustration.

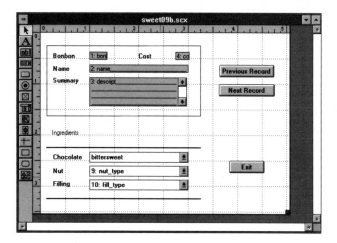

You might need to size some of the boxes so that all the text displays.

9 From the File menu, choose Save to store the work you have completed so far.

One Step Further

Currently, the Cost field allows the user to type the cost of the bonbon in the current record. To enable the user to take advantage of the mouse to make entries, you can create a spinner control. Using the up and down arrows on the spinner, the user can enter a new cost value.

Spinner tool

1 In the Screen Design window, select the Cost field and press DEL.

2 Click the spinner tool in the toolbox.

3 Click near where the Cost field was located.

The Spinner dialog appears.

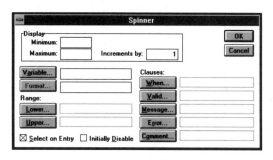

4 In the box next to the Variable push button, type **cost**

Specifying this field name ensures that whatever the user enters or selects in this field will be stored in the Cost field in the table. It also ensures that the contents of this field for the current record displays in the window.

5 In the Increments By box, type **.01**

This entry means that each time the user clicks the up or down arrow, the value in the field will increase (or decrease) by .01 (one cent).

You can leave the other settings in the Spinner dialog as they are.

6 Click the OK push button.

7 Size and position the Spinner control as needed.

Generate screen code

1 From the Program menu, choose Generate.

2 Click the Yes push button when you see the message asking whether you want to save changes to SWEET09B.SCX.

3 In the Generate Screen dialog, click the Generate push button.

After a moment, the code for your screen is generated and then stored in a file called SWEET09B.SPR.

Run the screen

1 From the Run menu, choose Screen.

The Open dialog appears.

2 In the Screen To Run list, select SWEET09B.SPR.

3 Click the Run push button.

The custom screen you created appears.

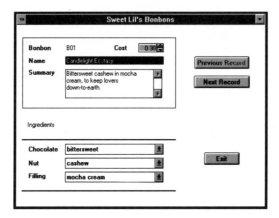

Experiment with the new controls on the screen by scrolling to different bonbon records and changing the characteristics of the bonbon. Adjust the cost with the spinner control.

4 Click the Exit push button to quit your custom screen when you are done.

If You Want to Continue to the Next Lesson

1 Click the Screen Design window to make it active.

2 From the File menu, choose Close.

If You Want to Quit FoxPro for Windows for Now

▶ From the File menu, choose Exit.

Lesson Summary

To	Do this
Create a new screen file	From the File menu, choose New. In the New dialog, click the Screen radio button. Click the New push button.
Use Quick Screen to create a custom screen	First, you must have a table open and be in the Screen Design window. From the Screen menu, choose Quick Screen. In the Quick Screen dialog, select the kind of screen layout you want, and then click the OK push button.
Adjust the screen size	Drag the lower-right corner of the screen.
Give the screen a title	From the Screen menu, choose Layout. In the Title box, type the title you want.
Center a screen	From the Screen menu, choose Layout. In the Position area, click the Center check box.
Make a display-only field	In the Screen Design window, double-click the field. In the Field area of the Field dialog, click the Output Field (Say) radio button. In the Options area, click the Refresh Output Field check box. Click the OK push button.
Cancel the screen program	From the Program menu, choose Cancel. Double-click the Control-menu box to close the window.

To	Do this
Create a push button	Click the Screen Design window to make it active. Click the push button tool. Click where you want to place the control. In the Push Button Prompts box, type the text you want to appear on the push button. Next to the variable push button, type a variable name, and then click the OK push button.
Create a popup	In the Screen Design window, click the popup tool in the toolbox. Click where you want to place the control. In the Popup dialog, enter each item you want to appear in the Popup Prompts list. Next to the Variable push button, type a field name, and then click the OK push button.
Generate screen code	From the Program menu, choose Generate. Click the Yes push button to save your changes. In the Generate Screen dialog, click the Generate push button.
Run a screen	From the Run menu, choose Screen. In the Screen To Run list, select the screen file you want to run. Click the Run push button.

For more information on	See in *Microsoft FoxPro for Windows Getting Started*
Creating a custom screen	Chapter 2, Quick Start
Screen Builder	Chapter 11, Designing a Custom Input Screen

For more information on	See in the *Microsoft FoxPro for Windows User's Guide*
Generating screen code	Chapter 6, Program Menu
Screen Builder	Chapter 11, Designing Screens with the Screen Builder

For more information on	See in the *Microsoft FoxPro for Windows Developer's Guide*
Creating screens	Chapter 2, Screens

Preview of the Next Lesson

In the next lesson, you will learn how to combine screens so that you do not have to create new push buttons that perform the same function in every custom screen. You will also learn how to add a FoxPro-style menu to give your custom screen the functions of a full-featured application.

Adding Capabilities to Your Screen

You can add features to your custom screens by displaying two screens at the same time. In addition, you can display your custom screen with a FoxPro-style menu and a control panel of push buttons.

In this lesson, you will modify a screen containing only push buttons, which can be used with almost any screen. Then you will combine this push button screen with a custom input screen. Finally, you will use the Application Generator to create a full-featured application consisting of a custom input screen, a control panel of push buttons, and a FoxPro-style menu.

You will learn how to:

- Display two screens at once.
- Generate an application with the Application Generator.
- Use the Application Generator menu with your application.
- Change screen object order.

Estimated lesson time: 35 minutes

If you closed FoxPro for Windows at the end of the last lesson

▶ Start FoxPro for Windows by double-clicking the FoxPro for Windows icon.

Creating a Utility Push Button Screen

As Sweet Lil's database application needs evolve, you realize that you will need to design and create more custom screens for this application. Each of these screens needs the Previous Record, Next Record, and Exit push buttons, as well as additional push buttons that display the first and last records in the database. You can save coding time and the possibility of errors by creating a utility push button screen that you will combine with other screens.

Open a screen file

1   From the File menu, choose Open.

The Open dialog appears.

2   In the List Files Of Type popup, select Screen.

3   In the Directory list, double-click PRACTICE to make it the current directory.

PRACTICE is already the current directory if you did not exit FoxPro for Windows at the end of the last lesson.

4   In the File Name list, select LSNS10A.SCX.

5   Click the Open push button.

The Screen Design window appears for this screen.

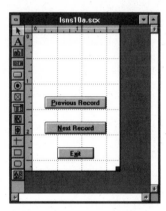

To reduce the amount of typing you have to do, start with a screen that already contains some of the push buttons you need. Before you combine this screen with another one, create additional useful push buttons. Your custom push button screen, called "Control Panel," will look like the following illustration.

Save the screen file with a new name

Before you make any changes to this file, save the file with a new name. By working in a copy of the file, you leave the original file intact so that you can repeat this exercise if you wish.

1   From the File menu, choose Save As.

The Save As dialog appears.

2   In the Save Screen As box, type **BUTTON10**

3   Click the Save push button.

Create a push button control

Create a push button control to display the first record in the table.

1   Click the push button tool.

2   Click the push button pointer just above the ½-inch grid line.

When you release the button, the Push Button dialog appears.

Push button tool

Modify the push button

Like the Previous Record push button you created in Lesson 9, this new push button contains a code snippet and uses a memory variable to store the results of the action.

1   In the Push Button Prompts box, type \<**First Record**

The "\<" indicates that the next character will be underlined on your push button, signifying a keyboard shortcut for the user. The user can simply type the letter instead of clicking the push button.

2   Click the Valid push button.

3   In the Code Snippet window, place the insertion point in the text box.

4   Type **go top**

This command selects the first record in the table when the user clicks this push button.

5   Press ENTER.

6   On the next line in the Code Snippet window, type **show gets**

The Show Gets command displays the information it gets after moving to the first record in the file.

7   Click the OK push button to return to the Push Button dialog.

8   In the box next to the Variable push button, type **m_first**

This stores the results of the action to a memory variable called "m_first."

Recall that you must assign a variable name or a field name to a control you create. So that the result of the action is not stored in the table, you need to assign a memory variable name to this push button.

9   Click the OK push button to return to the Screen Design window.

Push button tool

Create another push button

Create a push button control to display the last record in the table.

1   Click the push button tool.

2   Click the push button pointer just above the 1-inch grid line.

When you release the push button, the Push button dialog appears.

Modify the push button

1   In the Push Button Prompts box, type \\<**Last Record**

2   Click the Valid push button.

3   In the Code Snippet window, place the insertion point in the text box.

4   Type **go bottom**

This command selects the last record in the table when the user clicks this push button.

5   Press ENTER.

6   On the next line in the Code Snippet window, type **show gets**

The Show Gets command displays the information it gets after moving to the last record in the database.

7   Click the OK push button to return to the Push Button dialog.

8   In the box next to the Variable push button, type **m_last**

This stores the results of the action to a memory variable called "m_last."

9   Click the OK push button to return to the Screen Design window.

10   Adjust the size and position of the push buttons so that your screen looks like the following illustration.

Save the screen file

▶ From the File menu, choose Save.

Minimize the Screen Design window

▶ Click the Minimize button for the Screen Design window.

Modifying a Custom Input Screen

You plan to combine your push button screen with another screen. To minimize the amount of typing you have to do, you can start with a copy of a screen similar to the one you created at the end of Lesson 9 (SWEET09B.SCX). This screen does not contain any push buttons; however, it does contain the code snippets that use the variable names you have assigned to the push buttons in your custom screens. In addition, because this screen will be used as part of the application in which you can add records, the Bonbon_id field is now an input field.

Open a screen file

1   From the File menu, choose Open.

The Open dialog appears.

2   In the File Name list, select LSNS10B.SCX.

3   Click the Open push button.

The Screen Design window for this custom screen appears.

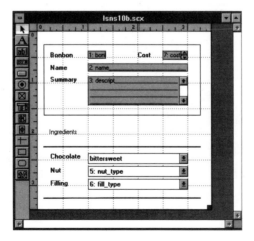

Save the screen file with a new name

Before you make any changes to this file, save the file with a new name. By working in a copy of the file, you leave the original file intact so that you can repeat this exercise if you wish.

1 From the File menu, choose Save As.

The Save As dialog appears.

2 In the Save Screen As box, type **SWEET10B**

3 Click the Save push button.

Combining Screens

You can combine screens easily in the Generate Screen dialog. The screens you combine here are displayed together the next time you run the generated screen program. Each time you want to see two custom screens at the same time, you will need to combine them in the Generate Screen dialog.

Open the Generate Screen dialog

▶ From the Program menu, choose Generate.

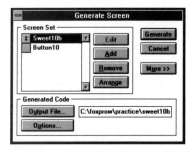

To combine a screen that is not currently open, click the Add push button. In the Add Screen dialog, double-click the screen you want to combine.

Because both of the screen files you combine are open right now, you see both screen file names (BUTTON10 and SWEET10B) in the Screen Set list.

Arrange the screens

1 In the Screen Set area, click the Arrange push button.

The Arrange Screens dialog appears.

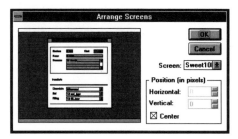

2 Clear the Center check box.

The SWEET10B screen moves to the left, revealing the BUTTON10 (Control Panel) screen under it.

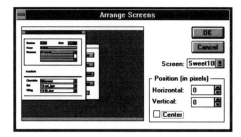

3 Click the Control Panel screen.

4 Clear the Center check box.

The BUTTON10 screen moves to the left.

5 Drag and position the two screens until the dialog looks like the following illustration.

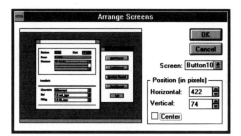

6 Click the OK push button to return to the Generate Screen dialog.

Generate screen code for the combined screens

▶ Click the Generate push button.

Close the Screen Design windows

1 Double-click the Control-menu box of the SWEET10B Screen Design window.

2 Restore the BUTTON10 Screen Design window by double-clicking its icon.

3 Double-click the Control-menu box of the BUTTON10 Screen Design window.

Run the screen

1 From the Run menu, choose Screen.

The Open dialog appears.

2 In the Screen To Run list, select SWEET10B.SPR.

3 Click the Run push button.

The custom windows appear.

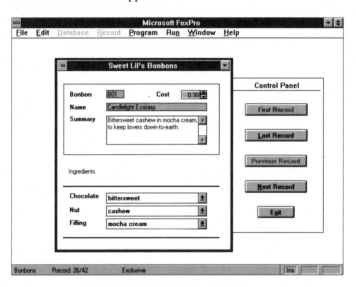

Experiment with the push buttons and controls in your new windows.

4 Click the Exit push button when you are done.

Generating an Application with the Application Generator

Adding push buttons is a convenient way to add a few operations to your screens. Common push buttons combined with custom screens add even more features and flexibility. However, requiring the user to click push buttons for every operation means a lot of coding for you and certain limitations for the user.

The custom screens you created for Sweet Lil's make it easy for the user to modify information in the bonbons database. But now you have learned that several users want to be able to add, copy, and delete records. They also want to create queries and reports. It will take a little time for you to add these operations to your application. Until then, you can use the Application Generator to add a simple FoxPro-style menu to your screen. The Application Generator also has a control panel containing push buttons similar to the ones you created earlier in this lesson. These features are sure to give your users the extra capabilities they want until you develop a custom menu in the next lesson.

Open a screen file

1   From the File menu, choose Open.

The Open dialog appears.

2   Be sure PRACTICE is the current directory shown above the Directory list.

If it is not the current directory, double-click PRACTICE in the Directory list.

3   In the File Name list, select LSNS10C.

4   Click the Open push button.

The Screen Design window for this screen appears.

Save the screen file with a new name

Before you make any changes to this file, save the file with a new name. By working in a copy of the file, you leave the original file intact so that you can repeat this exercise if you wish.

1   From the File menu, choose Save As.

The Save As dialog appears.

2   In the Save Screen As box, type **SWEET10C**

3   Click the Save push button.

4   Double-click the Control-menu box to close the Screen Design window.

Run the Application Generator

1   From the Run menu, choose Application.

The Open dialog appears.

2   Click the New push button.

The Application Generator dialog appears.

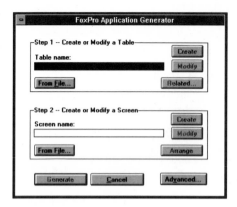

Enter the name of a table

1   In the Step 1 area, click the From File push button.

The Open dialog appears.

2   Be sure PRACTICE is the current directory shown above the Directory list.

If it is not the current directory, double-click PRACTICE in the Directory list.

3   In the Database Name list, select BONBONS.DBF.

This is the table with which your application will work.

4   Click the Open push button to return to the Application Generator dialog.

Enter the screen name for your application

1   In the Step 2 area, click the From File push button.

The Open dialog appears.

2   In the Screen File Name list, select SWEET10C.SCX.

This is the screen file with which your application will work. It is the one you saved before you started the Application Generator.

3   Click the Open push button to return to the Application Generator dialog.

Generate an application

1   Click the Generate push button.

The Save As dialog appears so you can provide a name for the application you are creating.

2   Click the Save push button to save this application with the same name as the screen, except with an APP extension.

After a few moments, all the code is gathered that is needed for your application. The application is complete when you see the following message.

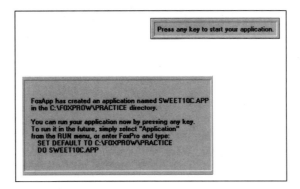

Run your application

▶ Press any key to run your application.

Your new application looks like the following illustration.

The Application Generator provides this menu.

The Application Generator provides this control panel.

Using the Menu with Your Custom Screen

The menu bar provided in the Application Generator for your application contains many of the options with which you are already familiar. For example, the Edit menu contains the Cut, Copy, and Paste options for editing fields. The Application menu, however, contains more options that provide new capabilities for managing and working with your data, such as creating queries and producing reports.

Because some of these options work a little differently than what you saw earlier, practice using your new application with its new menu.

Add a record

Sweet Lil's is adding a new line of liquor-flavored bonbons. Use the Add Record command to enter a new bonbon that is being developed at Sweet Lil's.

1   From the <u>A</u>pplication menu, choose <u>A</u>dd Record.

The Add Record command creates a new blank record at the end of the table. Because the current sort order is by bonbon ID, the blank record is displayed first in the list of records.

2   Enter the following information:

Bonbon	**L01**
Name	**Rum Raisin**
Summary	**Sweet raisins made plump with heady rum flavoring are enveloped in creamy centers and white chocolate.**
Chocolate	**white**
Nut	**none**
Filling	**special**
Cost	**.39**

Your window looks like the following illustration.

Leave the application

▶   From the <u>F</u>ile menu, choose <u>Q</u>uit to leave the custom application.

One Step Further

The sequence in which pressing TAB moves you between fields and controls in a window is called the *object order* (also known as *tab order)*. For example, when you reach the bottom of the screen, pressing TAB in the Filling field moves you to the Cost field at the top of the screen. Pressing TAB again moves you to the Bonbon_id field. The initial object order is determined by the order in which you create the objects. The number displayed with the field name reflects the current object order. For example, *1: bonbon_id* is the first field, *2: name* is the second, and so on.

To accommodate your users' data entry needs, you can change the object order so that the users can enter cost information immediately after entering bonbon ID information.

Open a screen file

1   From the File menu, choose Open.

The Open dialog appears.

2   In the List Files Of Type popup, select Screen.

3   Be sure PRACTICE is the current directory shown above the Directory list.

If it is not the current directory, double-click PRACTICE in the Directory list.

4   In the File Name list, select SWEET10B.

5   Click the Open push button.

The Screen Design window for this screen appears.

Change the object order

1   From the Screen menu, choose Object Order.

The Object Order dialog appears.

Drag the Mover button to move the Cost field here.

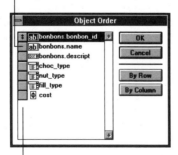

Drag the Mover button to move the Descript field here.

2 Drag the Mover button for the Cost field so this field appears just below Bonbon_id.

3 Drag the Mover button for the Descript field so that this field appears last in the list.

This placement allows the users to enter the ingredients for a bonbon before writing the description of the bonbon.

4 Click the OK push button.

Combine screens

1 From the Program menu, choose Generate.

2 Click the Yes push button when you see the message asking whether you want to save changes to SWEET10B.SCX.

3 Click the Add push button to add the Control Panel screen to this screen.

The Add Screen dialog displays.

4 Double-click BUTTON10.SCX.

Arrange the screens

1 Click the Arrange push button.

2 In the Arrange Screens dialog, clear the Center check box.

3 Drag the top screen to the left to reveal the Control Panel screen under it.

4 Select the Control Panel screen, and then clear the Center check box.

5 Drag and position the two screens until they are side by side.

6 Click the OK push button to return to the Generate Screen dialog.

Generate screen code for the combined screens

1 Click the Generate push button.

2 Click the Yes push button when you see the message asking whether you want to overwrite the existing SWEET10B.SPR file.

Run the screen

1 From the Run menu, choose Screen.

2 In the Screen To Run list, select SWEET10B.SPR.

3 Click the Run push button.

Experiment using TAB and SHIFT+TAB to move around the screen.

4 Click the Exit push button on the Control Panel to quit your custom screen when you are done.

If You Want to Continue to the Next Lesson

1   Click the Screen Design window to make it active.

2   From the File menu, choose Close.

If You Want to Quit FoxPro for Windows for Now

▶   From the File menu, choose Exit.

Lesson Summary

To	Do this
Combine screens	From the Program menu, choose Generate. Click the Yes push button when you see the message asking whether you want to save changes. Select the screens you want to add from the list of screens displayed in the Screen Set area. You can also click the Add push button to add a screen that is not open. Click the Generate push button to combine the screens.
Arrange screens (in the Generate Screen dialog)	From the Program menu, choose Generate. Click the Yes push button when you see the message asking whether you want to save changes. Click the Arrange push button. Clear the Center check box. Position the screens. Click the OK push button to return to the Generate Screen dialog. Click the Generate push button.
Run the Application Generator	From the Run menu, choose Application. In the Open dialog, click the New push button. In the Application Generator dialog, in the Step 1 area, click the From File push button. In the Database Name list, select the table with which your application will work. Click the Open push button. In the Step 2 area, click the From File push button. In the Screen File Name list, select the screen program file with which your application will work. Click the Open push button. Click the Generate push button.

For more information on	See in *Microsoft FoxPro for Windows Getting Started*
The Application Generator	Chapter 2, Quick Start

Preview of the Next Lesson

In the next lesson, you will learn how to create your own custom menus. By using the Menu Builder in FoxPro for Windows, you can create a menu that contains the commands and options you use most often. You will specify new option names and menu items that are unique to your application and your users' information needs.

Creating Custom Menus with the Menu Builder

When you use the Application Generator to generate an application based on your custom screen, a menu bar is generated that is an abbreviated version of the system menu bar (the FoxPro for Windows default menu system). The menu pads on this menu bar allow your users to perform basic operations in your application. To further customize FoxPro for your database management needs, you can create your own custom menus or modify existing ones.

In this lesson, you will use the Menu Builder to modify and enhance the menu in the Application Generator provided in Lesson 10. Your custom menu will contain the options your users require most often. You will also create hot keys so your users can use keyboard shortcuts to perform menu options. To make your menu easier to understand, you will specify messages to appear in the status bar. You will delete a menu pad and replace it with one you create. In addition, you will create your own popups. Finally, you will test your menu.

You will learn how to:

- Change menu prompts.
- Create hot keys.
- Create status bar messages.
- Delete a menu pad and its popup.
- Add a menu pad.
- Create popup menus.

Estimated lesson time: 45 minutes

If you closed FoxPro for Windows at the end of the last lesson

▶ Start FoxPro for Windows by double-clicking the FoxPro for Windows icon.

Understanding What Makes a Menu

Throughout this lesson, refer to the following illustration to identify the different parts of a menu.

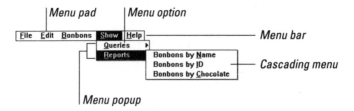

Menu element	Description
Menu bar	A bar across the top of the application window. The menu bar contains menu pads.
Menu pad	The name of each item on the menu bar. "File" is a menu pad.
Menu popup	A list of options that appears when you select a menu pad from the menu bar.
Cascading menu	A popup that displays another popup when you select it.
Menu option	An individual item on a menu popup. "New" is an option on the File menu popup.

Using the Menu Builder

In the Menu Design window, you specify each menu element you want for your menu. After you identify each of the menu pads that you want to appear on a menu bar, you need to define all the options you want to display on all the menu popups. You can build a custom menu from scratch in an empty Menu Design window, or you can use the Menu Design window to modify an existing menu file.

Note   You can also use Quick Menu to create a menu file that looks and acts like the FoxPro system menu.

Working in the Menu Design Window

You open the Menu Design window when you indicate that you want to create a new menu file in the New dialog, or when you open an existing menu file. To reduce the amount of typing you have to do in this lesson, you will modify an existing menu file.

Open the Menu Design window

1   From the File menu, choose Open.

The Open dialog appears.

2   In the List Files Of Type popup, select Menu.

3   In the Directory list, double-click PRACTICE to make it the current directory.

PRACTICE is already the current directory if you did not exit FoxPro at the end of the last lesson.

4   In the File Name list, select APPMENU.MNX.

5   Click the Open push button.

The Menu Design window appears.

This is the same menu file FoxPro provides when you use the Application Generator to create an application, as you did in Lesson 10. Although you can build a menu from scratch, it is more convenient to use an existing menu file as a starting point for designing your own custom menus.

Note   Because this file is part of a project file that you will modify in Lesson 12, do NOT change the file name.

Creating a Custom Menu

Sweet Lil's Manufacturing department has very specific information management requirements. So that they do not need special FoxPro training, the users in the department want their application's menus and popups to use terms with which they are already familiar. For example, the Application menu pad (which they want called "Bonbons") will have a menu popup with an option called "Add Bonbon," instead of "Add Record."

In addition, they want a quick way to show the results of the queries they use all the time. They want this capability on a menu pad called "Show"; the Show menu pad replaces the one currently called "Utilities." The menu popup for the Show menu will include Query and Report options; each in turn will display another menu popup with names of the queries (or reports) they want to do quickly. These queries and reports are implemented in Lesson 12.

When you begin this lesson, the menu for the Manufacturing department's application looks like the following illustration.

File   Edit   Application   Utilities   Help

After you change the Application menu pad and menu popup to the Bonbons menu pad and menu popup, your custom menu will look like the following illustration.

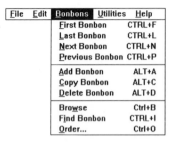

After you replace the Utilities menu pad and menu popup with the Show menu pad and menu popup, your custom menu will look like the following illustration.

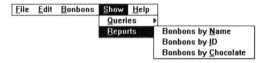

Specifying Menu Features

In the Menu Design window, you enter each menu pad name in the Prompt column. In the Result column, you identify what happens when your users select this menu pad. Your choices for results are listed in the following table.

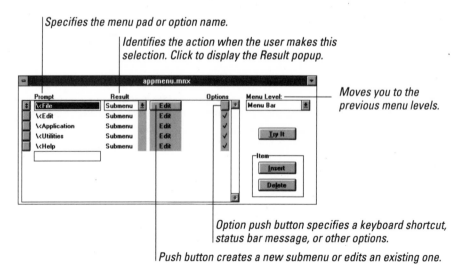

Specifies the menu pad or option name.

Identifies the action when the user makes this selection. Click to display the Result popup.

Moves you to the previous menu levels.

Option push button specifies a keyboard shortcut, status bar message, or other options.

Push button creates a new submenu or edits an existing one.

Result	Description
Submenu	Select this result to create a popup (either for a menu pad or for a cascading menu). Submenu is the default result.
Command	Select this result to execute a single command line when the user makes this selection.
Pad name	Select this result to execute a *system option* (an option found on the FoxPro system menu) when the user makes this selection.
Procedure	Select this result to execute more than one line of commands when the user makes this selection.

Depending on the result option you select, the column next to the Result column becomes either a text box or a Create push button. For example, if you select the Command result, the next column contains a text box in which you can enter the command you want to be executed. If you select a Submenu result, the next column becomes a Create push button that you click to define the popup for this menu pad. If a submenu is already defined, this push button becomes an Edit push button that you click to modify the submenu.

Setting Menu Options

There are two dialogs in which you specify characteristics and features of the custom menu. In the General Options dialog, you can enter a setup code snippet that executes after the new menu is displayed, but before the user selects an option. (You do not need to make any changes to the setup code snippet in this lesson.) In the Menu Bar Options dialog, you enter a code snippet for what you want to happen if the user selects an option for which there is no code.

Specify a menu bar procedure

Because you are designing and creating only the menu portion of your application in this lesson, a few of the selections do not do anything. In the Menu Options dialog, you can enter a procedure to display a "friendly message" when the user selects an option that you will not implement until later.

1   From the Menu menu, choose Menu Bar Options.

The Menu Options dialog appears.

2　Click in the Procedure text box to make it active.

3　Type **wait window "Feature not done (YET)"**

This code snippet displays a small message window when the user makes a selection for which there is no code. In the next lesson, you will attach the code that will make all the options on the menu popups perform useful tasks.

4　Click the OK push button.

Change a menu pad prompt option

In the Menu Design window, you modify the *prompts* (the words the users see on the menu bar or in a menu popup, such as File, New, Edit, Copy) for a custom menu.

1　In the Menu Design window, be sure the File prompt is selected.

2　Click the Options push button.

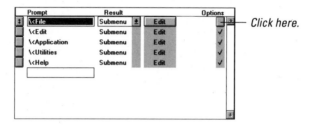
Click here.

The Prompt Options dialog appears.

3　Click the Message check box.

In the Expression Builder dialog, you can enter the message text you want displayed in the status bar when the user selects the File menu pad.

4　With the insertion point in the Message area, type **"Quit Bonbons"**

Be sure to include the quotation marks before and after the message text. They are required to display your message.

5　Click the OK push button to return to the Prompt Options dialog.

6　Click the OK push button to return to the Menu Design window.

Making Changes to Menu Popups

The users of your application will not use the Preferences option on the Edit menu popup. Delete this option (and the line above it) from this menu popup.

Modify a menu popup

1   Select the Edit prompt.

2   Click the Edit push button.

The prompts and results for the Edit menu popup appear in the Menu Design window.

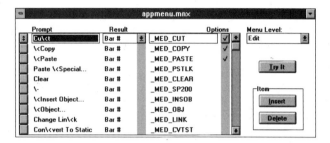

3   Select the prompt in the second to the last line, "\-"

The prompt "\-" creates a line in the menu popup that separates options from one another. Because you are removing the Preferences options, you also can remove the line above it.

4   In the Item area, click the Delete push button.

5   Click the Delete push button again to remove the Preferences option from the menu.

You have now removed the Preferences option and the line above it.

Changing Menu Levels

Menus are *hierarchical*. This means that when you are working with options on a menu popup, you need to return to the previous menu level before you can select another menu popup and work with its options. For example, because your current menu level is the Edit menu, you need to return to the Menu Bar level before you can specify options in the Help menu popup.

The current menu level appears in the Menu Level popup. You can use the Menu Level popup to select a menu level that is above the current level.

Change the menu level

▶   In the Menu Level popup, select Menu Bar.

The prompts and results for the menu bar appear.

Making More Changes to Menu Popups

The users of your application do not need the desk accessory options (such as Calculator and Calendar) on the Help menu popup. Delete these options from this menu popup.

Modify another menu popup

1   In the Menu Design window, click the Help prompt.

2   Click the Edit push button for the Help prompt.

The Menu Design window now contains the prompts and results for the Help menu popup.

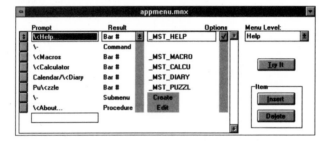

3   Select the prompt in the second line, "\-".

4   Click the Delete push button five times to remove each of the desk accessory options on the menu popup.

5   Click the Yes push button if you see the message asking whether you want to delete the submenu.

The Help menu popup now contains three prompts: Help, \-, and About.

6   From the File menu, choose Save.

Viewing Results

With the Try It push button, you can see the results of your changes and test your custom menu without generating menu code and running the menu. The Try It push button is a fast and convenient way to examine your menu.

Try it

1   Click the Try It push button.

2   Experiment with selections from the menu and menu popups.

The Try It dialog in the center of the window displays your selections, and the menu popups contain the options you modified. Your menu looks like the following illustration.

Help menu popup contains no desk accessory options.

3 Click the OK push button in the Try It dialog to return to the Menu Design window.

Customizing Another Menu Pad

The Application menu popup currently contains many of the options your users need to work with their bonbon records. To make your application *user-friendly* (that is, easy to use and understand), you can change the name of the menu pad and the names of the options that appear on the menu popup. You can also delete unnecessary options. After you complete the steps in this exercise, your menu will look like the following illustration.

```
File   Edit   Bonbons   Utilities   Help
              First Bonbon      CTRL+F
              Last Bonbon       CTRL+L
              Next Bonbon       CTRL+N
              Previous Bonbon   CTRL+P

              Add Bonbon        ALT+A
              Copy Bonbon       ALT+C
              Delete Bonbon     ALT+D

              Browse            Ctrl+B
              Find Bonbon       CTRL+I
              Order...          Ctrl+O
```

Change the menu level

▶ In the Menu Level popup, select Menu Bar.

The prompts and results for the menu bar appear.

Change a menu pad prompt

1 In the Menu Design window, click the Application prompt to make it active.

2 Double-click the word "Application."

3 Type **Bonbons**

"Bonbons" replaces the previous name on the menu pad to better identify this prompt. The "\<" specifies the keyboard equivalent for this menu pad and indicates that the character that follows (B) will be underlined.

Specify a keyboard shortcut

1 Click the Options push button.

2   In the Prompt Options dialog, click the Shortcut check box.

You need to click the check box (even if it is already checked) to display the Key Definition dialog.

3   In the Key Label box, press ALT+B.

This selection replaces the existing keyboard shortcut that is selected in the Key Label box. This specifies that the user can press ALT+B to select the Bonbons menu pad.

4   Click the OK push button.

Specify a message

1   In the Prompt Options dialog, click the Message check box.

In the Expression Builder dialog, you can enter message text to be displayed in the status bar when the user selects the Bonbons menu pad.

2   With the insertion point in the Message area, type:
"Add, Delete, and View Bonbons"

Be sure to include the quotation marks before and after the message text.

3   Click the OK push button to return to the Prompt Options dialog.

4   Click the OK push button to return to the Menu Design window.

Delete options from the menu popup

To be sure that your users will not see options they do not need, you can delete options from the menu popup.

1   In the Menu Design window, click the Edit push button for the Bonbons prompt.

The Menu Design window now contains the prompts and results for the Bonbons menu popup.

2   Select the C\<ycle prompt.

3   Click the Delete push button.

4   Select the Filter prompt.

You need to scroll downward to find it.

5   Click the Delete push button.

6   Select the separator prompt "\-" below the Order prompt.

7   Click the Delete push button five times to remove the remaining options (Pick \<list, \<Query, \<Report, and the two lines "\-") from the menu popup.

Modify an option's prompt

You can rename the Top option prompt.

▶   Triple-click the Top prompt, and type \<**First Bonbon**

Specify a keyboard shortcut

1   Click the Options push button.

2   In the Prompt Options dialog, click the Shortcut check box.

The Key Definition dialog appears.

3   In the Key Label box, press CTRL+F.

This selection replaces the existing keyboard shortcut that is selected in the Key Label box. This specifies that the user can press CTRL+F to select First Bonbon from the popup.

4   Click the OK push button to return to the Prompt Options dialog.

5   Click the OK push button to return to the Menu Design window.

Change other option prompts, shortcuts, and messages

Follow the same steps you used for changing the Top option to change the following prompts to reflect that the user is working with bonbon information.

Current prompt	New prompt	Shortcut
Bottom	\<Last Bonbon	CTRL+L
Next	\<Next Bonbon	CTRL+N
Prior	\<Previous Bonbon	CTRL+P
Add record	\<Add Bonbon	ALT+A
Copy record	\<Copy Bonbon	ALT+C
Delete record	\<Delete Bonbon	ALT+D

Note   The keys used in a keyboard shortcut can only be used for one operation. CTRL+A, CTRL+C, and CTRL+D are already used as keyboard shortcuts for other frequently used editing operations. You can retain these keyboard shortcuts by using ALT instead of CTRL in the keyboard shortcuts for the add, copy, and delete bonbon options.

Modify another option prompt

The Search option allows you to locate a specific record according to search criteria you specify. You can change this prompt to reflect that your users will search for a bonbon.

▶ Triple-click the Search prompt, and type **F\<ind Bonbon**

The "i" is used as the keyboard shortcut for this option.

Specify a keyboard shortcut

1 Click the Options push button.

2 In the Prompt Options dialog, click the Shortcut check box.

The Key Definition dialog appears.

3 In the Key Label box, press CTRL+I.

This specifies that the user can press CTRL+I to select Find Bonbon from the menu popup.

4 Click the OK push button.

5 Click the OK push button to return to the Menu Design window.

The Menu Design window looks like the following illustration.

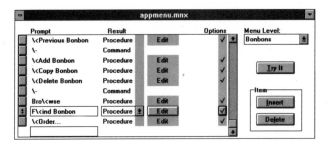

Try it

1 Click the Try It push button.

2 Experiment with making selections from the menu and popups.

The Try It dialog in the center of the window displays your selections.

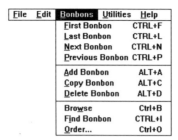

3   Click the OK push button in the Try It dialog to return to the Menu Design window.

Deleting a Menu Pad

The Utilities prompt does not contain the options the users need most often. Instead, the Manufacturing department wants a simple way to run queries and reports from the menu. Delete the Utilities menu pad and create a new menu pad. Then create a new menu popup that contains report and query options.

When you complete these steps, your menu will look like the following illustration.

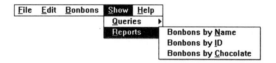

Change the menu level

▶   In the Menu Level popup, select Menu Bar.

The prompts and results for the menu bar appear in the Menu Design window.

Delete a menu pad

1   In the Menu Design window, select the Utilities prompt.

2   Click the Delete push button.

3   Click the Yes push button when you see the message asking whether you want to delete the submenu.

Creating a New Menu Pad and Menu Popup

In place of the Utilities menu pad you have just deleted, you can create a new menu pad called "Show." This menu pad will contain a menu popup that contains report and query options.

Create a new menu pad prompt

Be sure the Help menu pad is still selected.

1   Click the Insert push button.

2   In the Prompt column, type \<**Show**

This menu pad better reflects the options that will be available on the popup.

Specify a keyboard shortcut

1   Click the Options push button.

2   In the Prompt Options dialog, click the Shortcut check box.

The Key Definition dialog appears.

3   In the Key Label box, press ALT+S.

This specifies that the user can press ALT+S to select Show from the menu bar.

4   Click the OK push button.

Specify a message

1   In the Prompt Options dialog, click the Message check box.

The Expression Builder dialog appears.

2   With the insertion point in the Message area, type:
"Run Bonbon Queries and Reports"

Be sure to include the quotation marks before and after the message text.

3   Click the OK push button to return to the Prompt Options dialog.

4   Click the OK push button to return to the Menu Design window.

Add options to the popup

1   In the Menu Design window, click the Create push button for the Show menu popup.

2   In the Prompt column in the first line, type \<**Queries**

Specify the result

Your users want to choose from a list of three queries. You need to specify a result that presents another popup when your users select the Queries option.

▶   In the Result popup, be sure Submenu is selected.

    Submenu is the default result.

Enter another option prompt

▶   In the next blank line in the Prompt column, type \<**Reports**

Specify the result

Your users want to choose from a list of three reports. You need to specify a result that presents another popup when your users select the Reports option.

▶ In the Result popup, be sure Submenu is selected.

Creating Menu Popups for Options

The Submenu option allows you to create a menu popup. When you click the Create push button, you can enter the prompts and results for the menu popup. Adding a menu popup on a menu popup creates a *cascading menu* (sometimes called a submenu).

Create a popup option

1 Select the prompt for the Queries option.

2 Click the Create push button.

The Menu Design window clears the prompts and results for the Show menu pad. Now, you can enter prompts and results for the Queries option popup that will appear in a cascading menu.

3 In the Prompt column, type **Bonbons by \<Name**

4 In the Result popup, select Command.

5 In the next blank line of the Prompt column, type **Bonbons by \<ID**

6 In the Result popup, select Command.

7 In the next blank line of the Prompt column, type:
Bonbons by \<Chocolate

8 In the Result popup, select Command.

Create another popup option

1 In the Menu Level popup, select Show.

2 Select the prompt for the Reports option.

3 Click the Create push button.

The Menu Design window clears the prompts and results for the Show menu pad. Now, you can enter prompts and results for the Reports option popup that will appear in a cascading menu.

4 In the Prompt column, type **Bonbons by \<Name**

5 In the Result popup, select Command.

6 In the next blank line of the Prompt column, type **Bonbons by \<ID**

7 In the Result popup, select Command.

8 In the next blank line of the Prompt column, type:
Bonbons by \\<Chocolate

9 In the Result popup, select Command.

10 From the File menu, choose Save.

Try it

1 Click the Try It push button.

2 Experiment with making selections from the menu and menu popups.

Your selections appear in the Try It dialog in the center of the window. Your menu looks like the following illustration.

3 Click the OK push button in the Try It dialog to return to the Menu Design window.

One Step Further

Before you attach operations to your new menu, you want the manager of Manufacturing to take a look at your work that you completed so far. For your meeting in which you will demonstrate your menu, add a feature that identifies your application with the department that will use it.

The About option on the Help menu popup is usually used to display an About window. This window contains a brief description of the application. It often includes the application name, a version number, and other identifying information. Enter a command result to run an existing About window to provide this information.

Modify an option

1 In the Menu Level popup, select Menu Bar.

2 Select the prompt for the Help menu popup.

3 Click the Edit push button.

The prompts and results for the Help menu popup appear in the Menu Design window.

4 Select the About prompt.

5 Press TAB to move to the Result column.

6 Select Command from the popup.

7   Click the Yes button when you see the message asking whether you want to delete the existing procedure.

8   Press TAB to move to the text box.

9   Type **do aboutbox.spr**

This is a code snippet that runs the screen program that contains your About window. After you generate the project in Lesson 12, you can run the application and see the About window. The screen program for the About window is already provided on your exercise disk and was copied to the PRACTICE subdirectory.

If You Want to Continue to the Next Lesson

1   Double-click the Control-menu box in the Menu Design window to close it.

2   Click the Yes push button when you see the message asking whether you want to save your changes to APPMENU.MNX.

If You Want to Quit FoxPro for Now

1   From the File menu, choose Exit.

2   Click the Yes push button when you see the message asking whether you want to save your changes to APPMENU.MNX.

Lesson Summary

To	Do this
Start the Menu Builder	From the File menu, choose Open. In the List Files Of Type popup, select Menu. In the File Name list, select the menu file you want. Click the Open push button.
Specify a menu bar procedure	From the Menu menu, choose Menu Bar Options. Click in the Procedure text box to make it active. Type the code snippet. Click the OK push button.
Change a prompt option	In the Menu Design window, select the Prompt option you want to modify. Click the Options push button. In the Prompt Options dialog, click the Message check box. In the Expression Builder dialog, type your message text in the Message area.
Create a keyboard shortcut	In the Prompt Options dialog, click the Shortcut check box. In the Key Definition dialog, press the key or key combination that you want to be the shortcut. Click the OK push button.

To	Do this
Modify a menu popup	In the Menu Design window, select the prompt for the popup you want to change. Click the Edit push button. Modify the popup by changing prompts and by removing and adding options.
Change the menu level	In the Menu Level popup, select the menu level you want.
Delete a menu pad	In the Menu Design window, select the prompt you want to delete. Click the Delete push button. Click the Yes push button when you see the message asking whether you want to delete the submenu or procedure.
Create a new menu pad or option prompt	Click the Insert push button. In the Prompt column, type the new prompt. Arrange the prompts in the order you want.
Modify a popup option	Select the prompt for the menu pad of the popup you want to change. Click the Edit push button. Select the prompt you want to change. Press TAB to move to the Result column. Specify the new result.

For more information on	See in *Microsoft FoxPro for Windows Getting Started*
Customizing a menu	Chapter 12, Creating Your Own Menu System

For more information on	See in the *Microsoft FoxPro for Windows User's Guide*
Generating menu code	Chapter 6, Program Menu
The Menu Builder	Chapter 12, Designing Menus with the Menu Builder

For more information on	See in the *Microsoft FoxPro for Windows Developer's Guide*
Creating menus	Chapter 3, Menus
Screens and menus in an application	Chapter 4, Coordinating Screens and Menus

Preview of the Next Lesson

After you are satisfied with your menu, you need to regenerate the project file that the Application Generator created when you generated this application in Lesson 10. In the next lesson, you will use the Project Manager to add to and modify the list of files your application uses.

Putting It All Together with the Project Manager

The Application Generator in FoxPro for Windows prepares a project file that identifies all of the files (the menu file, screen files, procedures, reports, and queries) for your application. In this lesson, you will use the Project Manager to modify the project file that the Application Generator created for your application in Lesson 10. You will *build* your application (that is, generate application code) to incorporate the changes you made to the menu file in Lesson 11. Finally, you will use your custom application to add, copy, and delete records in the Bonbon database.

You will learn how to:

- Remove files from a project.
- Add new files to a project.
- Add code snippets to a project.
- Build an application.

Estimated lesson time: 45 minutes

If you closed FoxPro for Windows at the end of the last lesson

▶ Start FoxPro for Windows by double-clicking the FoxPro for Windows icon.

Understanding Projects and Applications

In FoxPro for Windows, an *application* is a collection of files (tables, screens, and menus) that work together to perform related database tasks, as seen from the perspective of the user. A *project* is this same group of files as seen by someone who develops an application.

In Lesson 10 and Lesson 11 you created two of the components you need for your custom application for the Manufacturing department at Sweet Lil's: You created a screen file that accepts input from your users, and you created a customized menu. When you create an application, you use the Project window to specify the files you want in your application so that these files can work together as a single program. When you save the project, you create a *project file*. This file contains references to all the files in the application. When you use the Application Generator to generate an application, this project file is created for you. If you add or modify any of the components in your application, you need to use the Project Manager to update the project file for your application.

You use the Project window when you open a new project file or when you modify an existing project file. After you complete this lesson, your Project window will look like the following illustration.

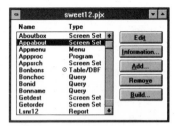

Open the Project window

1   From the File menu, choose Open.

The Open dialog appears.

2   In the List Files Of Type popup, select Project.

3   In the Directory list, double-click PRACTICE to make it the current directory.

PRACTICE is already the current directory if you did not exit FoxPro at the end of the last lesson.

4   In the File Name list, select SWEET10C.PJX.

5   Click the Open push button.

The Project window appears.

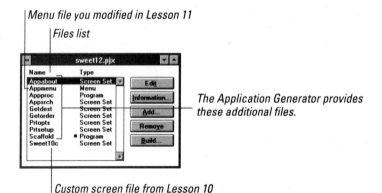

Menu file you modified in Lesson 11

Files list

The Application Generator provides these additional files.

Custom screen file from Lesson 10

This is the same project file the Application Generator created in Lesson 10. The Application Generator also provides the additional files it needs to make your application work. Although you can build a project from scratch, you can start with this project file to customize your application.

Note A *project file* contains the list of the files used in your application. An *application file* contains the code that allows all the files that are listed in the Project window to work together when the users run the application.

Save the project file with a new name

Before you make any changes to this file, save the file under a new name. By working in a copy of the file, you leave the original file intact so that you can repeat this exercise if you wish.

1 From the File menu, choose Save As.

The Save As dialog appears.

2 In the Save Project As box, type **SWEET12**

3 Click the Save push button.

Building an Application and Generating Code

In Lesson 11, one of the changes you made to the menu file APPMENU.MNX was to display a custom About window. To ensure that your application runs this revised menu file and can display the About window, you need to build the application and generate the code for your project.

Build the application

1 In the Project window, click the Build push button.

The Build Option dialog appears.

Click here.

2 Click the Build Application radio button.

3 Click the OK push button.

The Save As dialog appears.

4 Click the Build push button.

The name of the application file in which the application code is stored appears in the Enter Application Name text box. This name is based on the name of your project file. You can enter a different name if you wish, but it is easier to keep track of the project and application files if they both have the same name.

When the Project Manager finishes generating the code for your application, the Project window looks like the following illustration.

New screen file for custom About window

Notice that another file has been added to your application. The Aboutbox screen file contains the About window information. This file appears in the Project window because there is a code snippet in the menu file (in the About option on the Help menu popup) that refers to this file. As part of the building process, the Project Manager locates this file and supplies the filename in the Project window.

Exploring Your Project

After the code is generated, you can run your custom application. Once you are in the application, experiment with the buttons on the control panel to move through the records in the table. Then use the menu and the menu options to try out other features in the application.

Run your application

If the FoxPro logo is on the screen, you can get a better view of your application if you clear the logo first. From the Window menu, choose Clear.

1   From the Run menu, choose Application.

The Open dialog appears.

2   In the Application To Run list, select SWEET12.APP.

3   Click the Run push button.

Your screen looks like the following illustration.

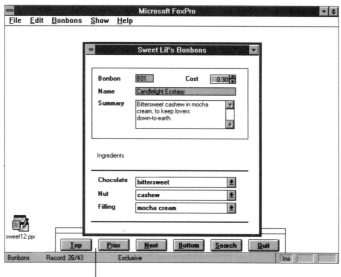

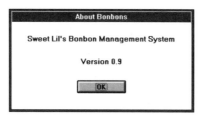

Control Panel provided by the Application Generator

Tip You can minimize the Project window if you wish. Remember to restore it to continue with the lesson.

Display information about your application

1 From the Help menu, choose About.

The About window appears.

```
┌──────────────────────────────┐
│       About Bonbons          │
├──────────────────────────────┤
│ Sweet Lil's Bonbon Management System │
│                              │
│        Version 0.9           │
│                              │
│          [OK]                │
│                              │
└──────────────────────────────┘
```

2 Click the OK push button to close the About window.

3 Experiment with the options on the other menu popups.

For the options that are not yet implemented, the Wait window displays the message "Feature not done (YET)."

Quit the custom application

There are two ways you can quit your custom application and return to the FoxPro system menu. You can use the Quit push button on the control panel, or you can use the Quit option from the File menu. Try both methods. Choose one option, and then run the application again and try the other.

▶ Click the Quit push button on the Control Panel.
   or
▶ From the File menu, choose Quit.

Working with Files in the Project Manager

The Project Manager keeps track of all the files your application uses and displays them in the list of files in the Project window. From the Project window it is easy to add, remove, and edit files in your application.

Remove a file from the project

When you build an application, the Application Generator automatically provides a file called Appabout, which displays an About window. Because your application uses your own About window, you can remove Appabout from the list of files in the Project window.

1 In the Project window, select Appabout.

2 Click the Remove push button.

3 Click the Yes push button when you are asked to confirm that you want to remove this file.

Because one of the files provided in the Application Generator references (but does not use) the Appabout file, the next time you build this project the Appabout file will appear again in the Project window.

Adding a Table

When you assemble files for a project, FoxPro specifies that the files in the Project window are *read-only* in your application. This means they can be executed but cannot be modified while the application is running. The Exclude option on the Project menu keeps a file from being read-only in your application.

Note   Specifying the table in a Project window is an optional step; your screen program already specifies and opens the correct table to use with your application. Nevertheless, specifically identifying the table in the Project window is a useful project maintenance technique to help a developer recall the table an application uses.

Add a table

Your application works with the BONBONS table. The data from this table is displayed when the user runs this application.

1   In the Project window, click the Add push button.

The Add File dialog appears.

2   In the List Files Of Type popup, select Table/DBF.

3   In the File To Add list, select BONBONS.

This is the table with which your application will work.

4   Click the Add push button.

The BONBONS table appears in the Project window.

5   With the BONBONS table still selected, from the Project menu, choose Exclude.

By using the Exclude option with your table, the user has the ability to update the BONBONS table.

Exclude symbol indicates this file is not "read-only." The user can update this table.

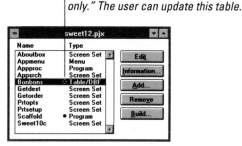

6   From the File menu, choose Save.

Implementing Show Menu Options

The Queries and Reports options on the Show menu popup are not implemented yet. You need to attach code snippets to these options in the Menu Design window so that when the user selects one of these options, the menu runs the correct query or report. Simple query and report files are provided in the PRACTICE directory, so you do not need to create them yourself.

Open the Menu Design window

1   In the Project window, select Appmenu.

2   Click the Edit push button.

The Menu Design window appears. This is the same menu file you modified in Lesson 11.

Add commands to query options

1   In the Menu Design window, select the prompt for the Show menu popup.

2   Click the Edit push button for the Show menu popup.

3   Click the Edit push button for the Queries option.

The prompts and results for the options on the Queries menu popup appear in the Menu Design window.

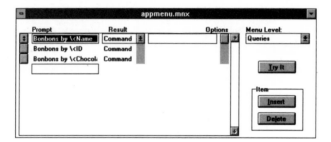

4   In the text box next to the Result column for the Bonbons By Name option, type **do bonname.qpr**

This code runs a query that displays bonbons ordered alphabetically by name.

5   Press the down arrow key to move to the text box for the Bonbons By ID option.

6   Type **do bonid.qpr**

This code runs a query that displays bonbons ordered alphabetically by bonbon ID.

7   Press the down arrow key to move to the text box for the Bonbons By Chocolate option.

8   Type **do bonchoc.qpr**

This code runs a query that displays bonbons ordered alphabetically by chocolate type.

9   From the File menu, choose Save.

Add commands to report options

1   From the Menu Level popup, select Show.

2   Select the prompt for the Reports menu.

3   Click the Edit push button for the Reports option.

The prompts and results for the options on the Reports menu popup appear in the Menu Design window.

4 In the text box next to the Result column for the Bonbons By Name option, type **do rbonname.qpr**

This code runs a query that produces a report of bonbons ordered alphabetically by name.

5 Press the down arrow key to move to the text box for the Bonbons By ID option.

6 Type **do rbonid.qpr**

This code runs a query that produces a report of bonbons ordered alphabetically by bonbon ID.

7 Press the down arrow key to move to the text box for the Bonbons By Chocolate option.

8 Type **do rbonchoc.qpr**

This code runs a query that produces a report of bonbons ordered alphabetically by chocolate type.

The Menu Design window looks like the following illustration.

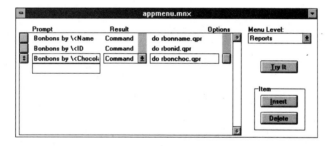

9 From the File menu, choose Save.

10 Minimize the Menu Design window.

Build the application

1 In the Project window, click the Build push button.

The Build Option dialog appears.

2 Be sure the Build Application radio button is still selected.

3 Click the OK push button.

The Save As dialog appears.

4 Click the Build push button.

5 Click the Yes push button when you see the message asking whether you want to overwrite the existing file.

When the Project Manager finishes generating the code for your application, the Project window looks like the following illustration.

Query files specified in the menu file

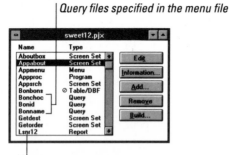

Report file used in the query

The queries you attached to the menu options now appear in the Project window. Scroll through the list of files to see other files added to the project.

Run your application

1 From the Run menu, choose Application.

The Open dialog appears.

2 In the Application To Run list, select SWEET12.APP.

3 Click the Run push button.

Your screen looks like the following illustration.

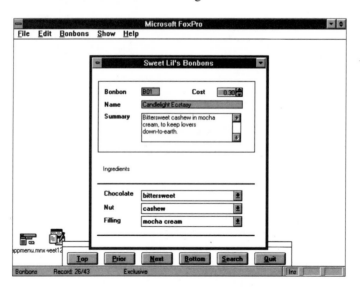

Generate a report

Experiment with the report options you just implemented.

1 From the Show menu, choose Report.

2 From the Report popup, choose Bonbons By Chocolate.

The report appears in the Page Preview window.

3 Click the OK push button to return to the custom window.

Search for a record

1 Click the Search button on the Control Panel.

FoxPro displays the Search For dialog.

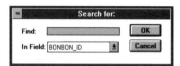

2 In the Find text box, type **Brazil**

3 Click the arrow in the In Field popup to display a list of fields from which you can choose.

4 Select **Nut_type**

5 Click the OK push button.

Your application displays the first record containing a brazil nut in the Nut_type field. A small message window in the upper-right corner contains the phrase "Found it!"

Re-establish display order

After you search for a record, the records are displayed in the order in which they were entered in the table. Use the Order option to display the records ordered by Bonbon ID.

1 From the Bonbons menu, choose Order.

The Order dialog appears.

2 In the Index Order popup, select Bonbon ID.

3 Click the OK push button.

Copy a record

Another new bonbon, a variation of the Brazilian Supreme, will have dark chocolate instead of white chocolate.

1 From the Bonbons menu, choose Copy Bonbon.

This command makes a copy of the current record immediately after its current location in the file. Your screen looks as though nothing has changed, but it actually has advanced to the next record (the duplicate record) in the file.

2 Change the bonbon ID to **D13**

3 Change the bonbon name to **Amazonian Supreme**

4 Change the summary text to:
A whole brazil nut hand-dipped in dark chocolate.

Memo fields are not copied.

5 Change the chocolate type from white to **dark**

Try other options

▶ Delete and add bonbons as you wish to try the new options.

Tip   You can delete records in the table, because they are not actually removed. To restore deleted records, leave the application, and then open the Command window and type:

use bonbons
recall all
use

When you press ENTER, the deleted records are restored to your table.

Leave the application

▶ From the File menu, choose Quit to leave the custom application.

One Step Further

As you saw in the previous step, the Copy Bonbon option does not copy the contents of the Descript memo field. By default, the command to copy records does not copy memo fields. However, there is a command that you can add to the Copy Bonbon code snippet that will include the memo field when you copy a record.

Modify the Copy Bonbon option code snippet

1 Double-click the Menu Builder icon at the bottom of the screen to restore the Menu Design window.

2 In the Menu Level popup, select Menu Bar.

3 Select the prompt for the Bonbons menu popup.

4 Click the Edit push button for the Bonbons menu pad.

5 Select the prompt for the Copy Bonbon popup.

6 Click the Edit push button for the Copy Bonbon option.

7 In the Copy Bonbon Procedure window, place the insertion point in the first line, after the SCATTER command.

8 Type **memo**

The first line in the window looks like the following illustration.

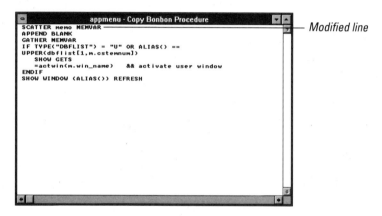

— Modified line

9 Place the insertion point at the end of the third line.

10 Type **memo**

The third line in the window looks like the following illustration.

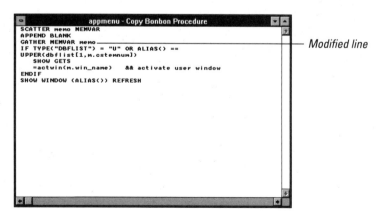

— Modified line

11   Close the code snippet window.

12   From the File menu, choose Save.

13   Close the Menu Design window.

Build the application

1   In the Project window, click the Build push button.

2   Be sure the Build Application radio button is still selected.

3   Click the OK push button.

4   Click the Build push button.

5   Click the Yes push button when you see the message to overwrite the existing file.

Run your application

1   From the Run menu, choose Application.

2   In the Application To Run list, select SWEET12.APP.

3   Click the Run push button.

4   Experiment with the Copy Bonbon option you just modified.

5   From the File menu, choose Quit to leave the custom application.

If You Want to Continue to the Review & Practice

▶   Close the Project window.

If You Want to Quit FoxPro for Now

▶   From the File menu, choose Exit.

Lesson Summary

To	Do this
Build the application	In the Project window, click the Build push button. Select the Build Application radio button. Click the OK push button. Click the Build push button in the Save As dialog. Be sure to rebuild the application anytime you make a change to the file listed in the Project window.

To	Do this
Add a file to the project	Click the Add push button. In the Add File dialog, select the type of file you want to add from the List Files Of Type popup. In the File To Add list, double-click the file you want to add. Click the Add push button.
Remove a file from the project	In the Project window, select the file you want to remove. Click the Remove push button.

For more information on	See in *Microsoft FoxPro for Windows Getting Started*
Developing your own applications	Chapter 13, Working with the Project Manager Chapter 14, Completing Your Application

For more information on	See in the *Microsoft FoxPro for Windows User's Guide*
Project Manager	Chapter 10, Building Projects with the Project Manager

For more information on	See in the *Microsoft FoxPro for Windows Developer's Guide*
Working with projects	Chapter 5, Project—The Main Organizing Tool
Troubleshooting an application	Chapter 6, Debugging Your Application

Review & Practice

The lessons in this part of the book showed you how easy it is to create your own custom applications using FoxPro power tools. The Review & Practice activity that follows will help you get ready to develop applications. This is a less structured scenario in which you can practice and refine your application development skills on your own. Follow the general guidelines—the rest is up to you.

Part 3 Review & Practice

In this Review & Practice section, you will practice the skills you learned in Part 3 by developing your own FoxPro for Windows custom application. You will start by developing a custom input screen. Then you will run the Application Generator with this screen and the EMPLOYEE table to generate an application. Using the menu file created by the Application Generator, you will change option names on the menu popups to customize the menu for the Human Resources staff. Finally, you will use the Project Manager to rebuild the application with the customized menu.

Scenario

In this Review & Practice section, you develop an application that Sweet Lil's Human Resources staff can use to manage employee information. Follow the general guidelines in each step. If you need help, use the table at the end of each step for references to additional information in the lessons.

You will review and practice how to:

- Create a custom screen.

- Run the Application Generator to create an application.

- Customize a menu.

- Use Project Manager to organize project files.

Estimated lesson time: 45 minutes

Step 1: Create a Custom Screen

In the Screen Design window, create a custom screen that has the features shown in the following illustration.

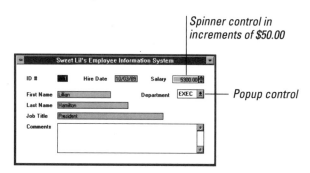

Open the EMPLOYEE table

▶ Use the View window to open a table called EMPLOYEE.DBF. This table is located in the REVIEW directory, so you need to double-click REVIEW in the Directory list of the Open dialog to display the list of tables.

Start the Screen Builder

From the File menu, choose New and indicate that you want to create a screen. With the Screen Design window open, choose Quick Screen from the Screen menu. Click the push button on the right, and then click the OK push button.

1   In the Screen Design window, arrange the fields as indicated in the sample screen.

2   Choose Layout from the Screen menu. In the Screen Layout dialog, specify the following:

- Center your screen.

- In the Title box, type **Sweet Lil's Employee Information System**

- In the Name field, type **EMPLOYEE**

- Click the Window Style push button. In the Window Style dialog, click the Close check box. Return to the Screen Layout dialog. Click the OK push button to return to the Screen Layout window.

3   Use the popup tool to create a popup control for the Department field. Enter the name of each of the following departments at Sweet Lil's in the Popup Prompts list:

EXEC
INFO
MANU
MRKT
OPER
SALE
SHIP

In the Variable text box, type **Employee.department**. Click the OK push button to return to the Screen Design window.

4   Use the spinner tool to create a spinner control for the Salary field. Use 50.00 for the increments field. In the Variable text box, type **Employee.salary**. Click the OK push button to return to the Screen Design window.

Generate the screen code

After you have designed your screen to look like the sample screen, you can generate the screen code.

▶ From the Program menu, choose Generate. In the Generate Screen dialog, click the Generate push button. Click the Yes push button when you see the message asking whether you want to save your changes to UNTITLED.SCX. In the Save dialog, be sure PRACTICE\REVIEW is the current directory. Save your screen file with the name REVS03.SCX. Click the Save push button to continue. Click the Yes push button when you see the message asking whether you want to save environment information with the screen.

Run the screen

1 From the Run menu, choose Screen. In the Open dialog, be sure PRACTICE\REVIEW is the current directory. Double-click your screen file, REVS03.SPR.

2 After you examine your window, from the Program menu, choose Cancel. Then double-click the Control-menu box on your custom window to close it.

3 Close the Screen Design window.

For more information on	See
Creating a Custom Screen	Lesson 9

Step 2: Create an Application with the Application Generator

Build an application based on the screen file you just created and the EMPLOYEE table.

Run the Application Generator

1 From the Run menu, choose Application. In the Open dialog, click the New push button.

2 In the Application Generator dialog, use EMPLOYEE.DBF as the table and REVS03.SCX as the screen file. Click the Generate push button. Click the Save push button in the Save As dialog to save the new application as REVS03.APP. Be sure PRACTICE\REVIEW is the current directory.

3 Try using your application after the Application Generator completes generating your application.

For more information on	See
Using the Application Generator	Lesson 10

Step 3: Customize a Menu

So that the Human Resources staff can use your application without learning special FoxPro for Windows terminology, change the option names on the menu popups provided by the Application Generator, according to the table in Step 2 of the following procedure.

Start the Menu Builder

1   From the File menu, choose Open. In the Open dialog, double-click PRACTICE\REVIEW as the current directory. From the List Files Of Type popup, select Menu. From the File Names list, double-click APPMENU.MNX.

2   In the Menu Design window, make the following changes to the menu popups and options:

Change	To
Application	Employees
Add Record	Add Employee
Copy Record	Copy Employee
Delete Record	Remove Employee

3   Remove Queries from the Application menu popup. Create a Queries menu pad and menu popup to replace the Utilities menu pad.

4   Add two queries to the Queries menu pad:

Filename	Menu pad name
REVQEMPL.QPR	Employees By Name
REVQDEPT.QPR	Employees By Department

5   Save your work by choosing Save from the File menu.

6   Close the Menu Design window.

For more information on	See
Using the Menu Builder	Lesson 11

Step 4:   Use the Project Manager to Build the Application

After making modifications to the menu file, you need to rebuild the application. Rebuilding the application also adds the query files to the project list.

Start the Project Manager

1   From the File menu, choose Open. In the List Files Of Type popup, select Project. In the File Name list, double-click REVS03.PJX. This is the project file the Application Generator generated for you in Step 2.

2   In the Project window, choose the Build push button. Be sure the Build Application radio button is selected in the Build Option dialog. Click the OK push button to generate the application. In the Save As dialog, click the Build push button. Click the Yes button when you see the message asking whether you want to overwrite the existing file.

When the Project Manager completes building the application, the query files you added in the last step appear in the Project window.

3   Experiment using your new Employee application.

Tip Because query results display in the active window, be sure the custom window is the active window when you select a query option.

If You Want to Quit FoxPro for Windows for Now

1 Click the Quit push button on the Control Panel.

2 From the File menu, choose Exit.

For more information on	See
Building an Application and Generating Code	Lesson 12

Appendix

Clarifying Code Snippets

This appendix contains additional information about the code snippets used in the screen files provided on the practice disk. These code snippets minimized the amount of typing you had to do when you created a popup control, and they prevented screen failures caused by trying to use push buttons at the wrong time. This material is not included in the Step by Step activities because it is not basic FoxPro for Windows information and is outside the scope of this book.

However, if you plan to go beyond the basics and develop custom applications, it is useful know how these code snippets work so that you can use them in your own applications.

Using an Array in a Popup Control

As you learned in Lesson 9, an array is a memory variable that contains multiple items. When you created the nut-type and filling-type popup controls, you could have entered each item in the Popup Prompts List. Instead you specified the name of an array. The arrays included in the screen setup code snippet contain a list of nut types and filling types that appear in the popups when you run the screen program. Arrays have two important benefits:

- When you want to use the same list of items for another control, you can simply specify the array name, rather than type in each item. This is especially helpful when the popup list contains many items.

- If an item in the list changes, you only have to edit the item in the array rather than the item in each individual popup list where the item is used.

To use an array in a control, you need to *dimension* the array in the screen setup code of the screen containing the control. Dimensioning an array means giving the array a name and specifying the number of items in the array. After you dimension the array, you list each of the individual items in the array. Here are the two arrays you used in Lesson 9. The code snippets for these arrays are included in each of the screen files you used in the remaining lessons.

You can see the code for these arrays in the screen setup code snippet window for any of these screen files:

- LSNS09b, SWEET09b
- LSNS10b, SWEET10b
- LSNS10c, SWEET10c

Nut-Type Array

This array contains the nine nut-type selections that appear in the nut-type popup control in the Bonbons application screens.

Code	Explanation
dimension m_nuttypes(9)	Dimensions the array by specifying the variable name "m_nuttype" and indicating that there are nine items in this array.
store "almond" to m_nuttypes(1)	Stores the text "almond" to the first location in the array.
store "brazil" to m_nuttypes(2)	Stores the text "brazil" to the second location in the array.
store "cashew" to m_nuttypes(3)	Stores the text "cashew" to the third location in the array.
store "hazelnut" to m_nuttypes(4)	Stores the text "hazelnut" to the fourth location in the array.
store "macadamia" to m_nuttypes(5)	Stores the text "macadamia" to the fifth location in the array.
store "none" to m_nuttypes(6)	Stores the text "none" to the sixth location in the array.
store "pecan" to m_nuttypes(7)	Stores the text "pecan" to the seventh location in the array
store "pistachio" to m_nuttypes(8)	Stores the text "pistachio" to the eighth location in the array.
store "walnut" to m_nuttypes(9)	Stores the text "walnut" to the ninth location in the array.

Filling-Type Array

This array contains the 14 fill-type selections that appear in the filling-type popup control in the Bonbons application screens.

Code	Explanation
dimension m_filltypes(14)	Dimensions the array by specifying the variable name "m_filltype" and indicating that there are 14 items in this array.
store "amaretto" to m_filltypes(1)	Stores the text "amaretto" to the first location in the array.
store "blueberry" to m_filltypes(2)	Stores the text "blueberry" to the second location in the array.
store "cherry cream" to m_filltypes(3)	Stores the text "cherry cream" to the third location in the array.

Code	Explanation
store "cherry, whole" to m_filltypes(4)	Stores the text "cherry, whole" to the fourth location in the array.
store "coconut" to m_filltypes(5)	Stores the text "coconut" to the fifth location in the array.
store "fondant" to m_filltypes(6)	Stores the text "fondant" to the sixth location in the array.
store "marmalade" to m_filltypes(7)	Stores the text "marmalade" to the seventh location in the array.
store "marzipan" to m_filltypes(8)	Stores the text "marzipan" to the eighth location in the array.
store "mocha cream" to m_filltypes(9)	Stores the text "mocha cream" to the ninth location in the array.
store "none" to m_filltypes(10)	Stores the text "none" to the tenth location in the array.
store "peanut butter" to m_filltypes(11)	Stores the text "peanut butter" to the eleventh location in the array.
store "raspberry" to m_filltypes(12)	Stores the text "raspberry" to the twelfth location in the array.
store "special" to m_filltypes(13)	Stores the text "special" to the thirteenth location in the array.
store "strawberry" to m_filltypes(14)	Stores the text "strawberry" to the fourteenth location in the array.

Enabling and Disabling Push Buttons

As you saw in Lesson 9, the screen program failed when you attempted to display a previous record when the current record was the first record in the table. Similarly, the screen program failed when you attempted to display the next record when the current record was the last record in the table.

The screen files LSNS09b, SWEET09b, LSNS10b, and SWEET10b contain code snippets (in the Screen Setup clause and in the On Refresh (Show Gets) clause) to enable and disable these push buttons (as well as the First Record and Last Record push buttons) when appropriate. Be aware that these clauses must contain these code snippets for any custom screen that you create in which you use controls to perform these operations.

Screen Setup Code Snippet

The Screen Setup clause contains the following code snippet, which stores the record number of the first and last records in memory variables.

Code	Explanation
go bottom	Moves to the end of the table.
store recno( ) to m_bottom	Stores the current record number to a variable called "m_bottom."
go top	Moves to the beginning of the table.
store recno( ) to m_top	Stores the current record number to a variable called "m_top."

The code also ensures that the first record in the table always appears first when the user runs the application.

On Refresh (Show Gets) Code Snippet

The On Refresh (Show Gets) clause contains code that tests to see if the current record number is equal to the values in either of the memory variables, m_top and m_bottom. If the current record number is equal to the record number for the first record, the First Record and Previous Record push buttons are disabled (while the Last Record and Next Record push buttons are enabled); thus the program is prevented from failing in the manner you saw in Lesson 9.

Similarly, if the current record number is equal to the record number for the last record, the Last Record and Next Record push buttons are disabled (while the First Record and Previous Record push buttons are enabled).

The On Refresh (Show Gets) code snippet to disable/enable the Previous Record and First Record push buttons looks like the following.

The code between the IF and ENDIF commands is called an IF structure. Indenting the code inside the IF structure is an optional formatting convention that makes the code easier to read and understand.

Code	Explanation
if (recno( ) = m_top)	This code tests to see if the current record number is equal to m_top (the record number of the first record).
show get m_prev disable *show get m_first disable*	If it is, this code disables the Previous Record and the First Record push buttons. You gave these push buttons the variable names "m_prev" and "m_first" when you first created them.
else	Otherwise, if the current record number is not equal to m_top (the first record), then
show get m_prev enable *show get m_first enable*	Enable the Previous Record and First Record push buttons.
endif	Ends IF structure.

The On Refresh (Show Gets) code snippet to disable/enable the Next Record and Last Record push buttons looks like the following.

Code	Explanation
if (recno( ) = m_bottom)	This code tests to see if the current record number is equal to m_bottom (the record number of the last record).
show get m_next disable *show get m_last disable*	If it is, this code disables the Next Record and Last Record push buttons. You gave these push buttons the variable names "m_next" and "m_last" when you first created them.
else	Otherwise, if the current record number is not equal to m_bottom (the last record), then
show get m_next enable *show get m_last enable*	Enable the Next Record and Last Record push buttons.
endif	Ends IF structure.

Glossary

active window   The window in which the next action takes place. When several windows are open, the active window is the top window on the desktop. You can click a window to make it active.

alias   The name assigned to a table. When a field name is fully qualified, the alias of the table precedes the field name.

AND   The operator requiring that all conditions must be met to be included in selection criteria.

application   A collection of FoxPro for Windows files (menus, screens, and tables) integrated together (with a program or the Application Generator) to perform a specialized purpose. See also *project*.

arguments   Additional information or parameters with which a function works, usually enclosed in parentheses following the function name. For example, the PADR() function in PADR(CA,10) contains two arguments: CA and 10.

array   A single memory variable containing multiple items in a list within the array. Items in the array are referred to by their numbered position in the array. An array is specified in a code snippet or program.

Browse window   The window in which table information is displayed in rows and columns, as found in a spreadsheet.

bug   A condition in a program or code snippet causing a result that was not intended.

CDX file   A structural compound index file. It is often called a CDX file because a structural compound index file has the extension CDX.

case-sensitive   The ability to distinguish between uppercase and lowercase text. For example, the Exactly Like comparison operator is case-sensitive, because it considers the case of the selection criteria when evaluating data. On the other hand, the Like comparison operator is not case-sensitive, because it ignores the case of the selection criteria when evaluating data.

character field   A field type containing text that is not a numeric value representing a quantity or used in a calculation.

check box   A control in the shape of a square box that represents an option in a dialog. A check box is selected if it contains an "X." Clicking the "X" in the check box clears it. In some cases, clicking a check box displays another dialog.

child table   A table that is subordinate to a parent table; the second table specified in a field relationship.

clause   An additional code statement that follows a command or a function. Clauses contain code snippets for menus, screens, and screen objects.

code snippet   A short sequence of commands that affects the operation of menus, screens, and controls.

command   An instruction in a program or in the Command window that causes the application to perform an action.

Command window   The window in which you can enter FoxPro language commands. Commands also appear in the Command window when you make selections from a menu.

comparison operator   The expression used to compare a value in a field with the selection criteria. The comparison operators in the RQBE window are More Than, Less Than, Like, Exactly Like, Between, and In.

control   An item in a dialog or a window that requires the user to perform an action to proceed. Check boxes, list boxes, popups, push buttons, and radio buttons are controls.

current directory   The active directory in the Open dialog where the files in the File Name list are stored; the directory in which the next action will take place. You can double-click a directory to make it the current directory. The name of the current directory appears above the Directory list in the Open dialog.

database   A collection of related information, organized for easy retrieval. See also *table*.

data grouping   Records containing similar information grouped together, usually in a report.

data type   The kind of data a field can contain. Data types are character, numeric, float, logical, memo, and date.

date field   A field type that contains a date.

debug   The process of identifying and correcting errors (bugs) in code and/or logic in a program or code snippet.

default   A pre-existing condition or setting. Unless you specify otherwise, the default condition occurs automatically.

dialog   The FoxPro for Windows term for dialog box. Dialogs contain the controls and options to which you respond to complete an operation.

disabled   A control or option that is dimmed and not available for use.

enabled   A control or option that is available for use.

Expression Builder   A FoxPro for Windows feature that allows you to combine fields, variables, operators, and functions to create expressions.

field   A single item of data in a table; a part of a record.

field object   An item in a report or a screen that reflects data found in a field.

FoxApp   In earlier versions of FoxPro, this was the name for the Application Generator power tool.

function   A special command providing a value that is the result of performing an action.

graphic object   A line or box in a report or screen.

group band   An area in the Report Layout window containing data pertaining to a *data grouping*. A group band appears with each group of data in a report.

index file   A file containing a list of index keys reflecting the ways in which records in a table can be ordered.

index key   The field expression by which records in a table can be ordered. See also *tag* and *tag name*.

join condition   The common field between two tables, specifying the relationship between the tables.

keyboard equivalent   The keystrokes you can use to make a menu bar or menu popup selection without using the mouse.

keyboard shortcut   The key combination you can use to bypass the menu bar and select an option without using the mouse.

logical field   A field type that contains only a true or a false value.

marquee   The dotted box that appears when you drag the pointer around a group of objects to select them.

memo field   A field type that contains free-form text of unlimited length.

memory variable   A named temporary location in computer memory that contains data. Usually used in code snippets or when creating screen controls.

menu bar   The horizontal list of menu pads displayed at the top of the FoxPro for Windows application window.

menu option   A command displayed on a menu popup that you can select to perform an action.

menu pad   The item (menu name) on the menu bar.

menu popup   A list of the options that appears when you select a menu pad.

numeric field   A field type containing numbers that are used in calculations.

object   An item in FoxPro for Windows graphical tools (Report Writer and Screen Builder) that you can select, move, and size.

object order   The order in which the selection moves from control to control or field to field when you press TAB in a screen. Sometimes called *tab order*.

OR   An operator specifying that a record must match the selection criteria that either precedes or follows the OR operator.

pack   Permanently removes from a table any records marked for deletion.

page footer band   An area of the Report Layout window containing data that will appear at the bottom of every page in a report.

page header band   An area of the Report Layout window containing data that will appear at the top of every page in a report.

parameter   Another term for *argument*.

parent table   A table that controls a subordinate (child) table.

popup   A list of options that appears when you make a selection in a dialog or when you select an option.

power tool   One of several FoxPro for Windows tools that makes FoxPro easier to use and increases productivity. FoxPro for Windows power tools include: Report Writer, RQBE, Screen Builder, Application Generator, Menu Builder, and Project Manager.

program   A series of instructions (commands) performed in a sequence specifying actions to accomplish a task. See also *code snippet*.

project   A list of files needed to run an application, created using the Project Manager or the Application Generator.

query file   A file that contains the RQBE specifications regarding selection criteria, output fields, and results output.

record   A collection of fields related to a specific item in a table.

refresh   Clears existing data from screens or fields to display new data.

related table   A child table related to a parent table.

RQBE   Relational Query By Example. The method in which you specify query specifications by entering selection criteria with example data in the RQBE window.

screen set   A file containing two or more screen files.

selection   The data or items that are affected by the next action. A selection is highlighted on the screen.

setup code   Code that is executed before a menu or screen appears.

string   A group of text characters, as in a character field.

structural compound index   An index file that has the same name as the original file, except with a CDX extension. This file is opened at the same time the original file.

summary band   An area of the Report Layout window containing data pertaining to all the records in a report. A summary band appears at the end of a report.

system menu   The default menu system in FoxPro for Windows (menu bar, menu pads, and menu popups).

tab order   See *object order*. See also *index key*.

table   Related information organized in records and fields.

tag   Another name for index key. See also *index key*.

tag name   The name that identifies the index key.

user   Someone who uses an application. In this book, the user is someone for whom you are developing an application.

work area   The area in which you work with an individual table. Only one table can be open in a work area. To work with more than one table, you can open additional tables in other work areas.

view file   The file in which settings in the View window are stored. The view file specifies table relationships, index keys, and sort orders.

Index

Note: Italicized page numbers refer to illustrations.

F

Catapult, Inc.

Catapult is a national software training company dedicated to providing the highest quality application software training. Years of PC and Macintosh instruction for major corporations and government institutions provide the models used in building Catapult's exclusive Performance-Based Training program. Based on the principles of adult learning, Performance-Based Training materials ensure that training participants leave the classroom with the ability to apply skills acquired during the training day.

Catapult's Curriculum Development group is pleased to share their training skills with a wider audience through the Step by Step series. FoxPro for Windows is the third in the Step by Step series to be produced by Catapult Press. This book and others in the series will help you develop the confidence necessary to achieve increased productivity with your Microsoft products.

Catapult's corporate headquarters are in Bellevue, Washington.

STEP BY STEP SERIES
The Official Microsoft® Courseware

These timesaving book-and-disk packages from Microsoft Press are the official courseware
for Microsoft's top-selling software. Geared for time-sensitive individuals new to the software but
with some computer experience, they offer excellent self-paced instruction through disk-based tutorials,
follow-along lessons, and practice exercises. All the lessons are illustrated with examples and are fully integrated
with the practice files on disk—ideal for professional training in the classroom or for
home use. There's no downtime or lost productivity because users learn right at their own desks.
It's the perfect solution for today's on-the-go businesspeople.

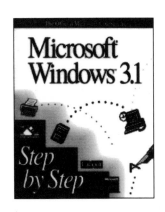

MICROSOFT® WINDOWS™ 3.1
STEP BY STEP

Catapult, Inc.

Learn Microsoft Windows quickly and easily with
MICROSOFT WINDOWS 3.1 STEP BY STEP.

296 pages, softcover with one 3.5-inch disk
$29.95 ($39.95 Canada)   ISBN 1-55615-501-8

MICROSOFT® WORD FOR WINDOWS™
STEP BY STEP

Microsoft Corporation

Learn to produce professional-quality documents with ease.
Covers version 2.

296 pages, softcover with one 5.25-inch disk
$29.95 ($39.95 Canada)   ISBN 1-55615-467-4

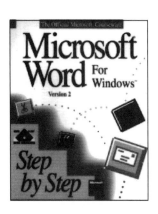

MICROSOFT® EXCEL FOR WINDOWS™
STEP BY STEP, 2nd ed.

Microsoft Corporation

Become a spreadsheet expert the easy way!
Covers version 4.0.

336 pages, softcover with one 3.5-inch disk
$29.95 ($39.95 Canada)   ISBN 1-55615-476-3

MICROSOFT® EXCEL MACROS
STEP BY STEP

Steve Wexler and Julianne Sharer
for WexTech Systems, Inc.

Create effective and efficient macros with Microsoft
Excel version 4.0 for Windows™ and the Apple® Macintosh.®

272 pages, softcover with two 3.5-inch disks
$34.95 ($47.95 Canada)   ISBN 1-55615-496-8

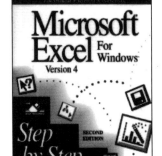

Microsoft Press books are available wherever quality computer books are sold. Or call 1-800-MSPRESS for ordering
information or for placing credit card orders. Please refer to BBK when placing your order. Prices subject to change.*
In Canada, contact Macmillan Canada, Attn: Microsoft Press Dept., 164 Commander Blvd., Agincourt, Ontario, Canada M1S 3C7, or call (416) 293-8141.

In the U.K., contact Microsoft Press, 27 Wrights Lane, London W8 5TZ. All other international orders will be forwarded to the appropriate distributor.

IMPORTANT — READ CAREFULLY BEFORE OPENING SOFTWARE PACKET(S).

**By opening the sealed packet(s) containing the software, you indicate your acceptance
of the following Microsoft License Agreement.**

Microsoft License Agreement

MICROSOFT LICENSE AGREEMENT
(Single User Products)

This is a legal agreement between you (either an individual or an entity) and Microsoft Corporation. By opening the sealed software packet(s) you are agreeing to be bound by the terms of this agreement. If you do not agree to the terms of this agreement, promptly return the book, incuding the unopened software packet(s), to the place you obtained it for a full refund.

MICROSOFT SOFTWARE LICENSE

1. GRANT OF LICENSE. Microsoft grants to you the right to use one copy of the Microsoft software program included with this book (the "SOFTWARE") on a single terminal connected to a single computer. The SOFTWARE is in "use" on a computer when it is loaded into temporary memory (i.e. RAM) or installed into permanent memory (e.g., hard disk, CD-ROM, or other storage device) of that computer. You may not network the SOFTWARE or otherwise use it on more than one computer or computer terminal at the same time.

2. COPYRIGHT. The SOFTWARE is owned by Microsoft or its suppliers and is protected by United States copyright laws and international treaty provisions. Therefore, you must treat the SOFTWARE like any other copyrighted material (e.g., a book or musical recording) except that you may either (a) make one copy of the SOFTWARE solely for backup or archival purposes, or (b) transfer the SOFTWARE to a single hard disk provided you keep the original solely for backup or archival purposes. You may not copy the written materials accompanying the SOFTWARE.

3. OTHER RESTRICTIONS. You may not rent or lease the SOFTWARE, but you may transfer the SOFTWARE and accompanying written materials on a permanent basis provided you retain no copies and the recipient agrees to the terms of this Agreement. You may not reverse engineer, decompile, or disassemble the SOFTWARE. If the SOFTWARE is an update or has been updated, any transfer must include the most recent update and all prior versions.

4. DUAL MEDIA SOFTWARE. If the SOFTWARE package contains both 3.5" and 5.25" disks, then you may use only the disks appropriate for your single-user computer. You may not use the other disks on another computer or loan, rent, lease, or transfer them to another user except as part of the permanent transfer (as provided above) of all SOFTWARE and written materials.

5. LANGUAGE SOFTWARE. If the SOFTWARE is a Microsoft language product, then you have a royalty-free right to reproduce and distribute executable files created using the SOFTWARE. If the language product is a Basic or COBOL product, then Microsoft grants you a royalty-free right to reproduce and distribute the run-time modules of the SOFTWARE provided that you: (a) distribute the run-time modules only in conjunction with and as a part of your software product; (b) do not use Microsoft's name, logo, or trademarks to market your software product; (c) include a valid copyright notice on your software product; and (d) agree to indemnify, hold harmless, and defend Microsoft and its suppliers from and against any claims or lawsuits, including attorneys' fees, that arise or result from the use or distribution of your software product. The "run-time modules" are those files in the SOFTWARE that are identified in the accompanying written materials as required during execution of your software program. The run-time modules are limited to run-time files, install files, and ISAM and REBUILD files. If required in the SOFTWARE documentation, you agree to display the designated patent notices on the packaging and in the README file of your software product.

LIMITED WARRANTY

LIMITED WARRANTY. Microsoft warrants that (a) the SOFTWARE will perform substantially in accordance with the accompanying written materials for a period of ninety (90) days from the date of receipt, and (b) any hardware accompanying the SOFTWARE will be free from defects in materials and workmanship under normal use and service for a period of one (1) year from the date of receipt. Any implied warranties on the SOFTWARE and hardware are limited to ninety (90) days and one (1) year, respectively. Some states/countries do not allow limitations on duration of an implied warranty, so the above limitation may not apply to you.

CUSTOMER REMEDIES. Microsoft's and its suppliers' entire liability and your exclusive remedy shall be, at Microsoft's option, either (a) return of the price paid, or (b) repair or replacement of the SOFTWARE or hardware that does not meet Microsoft's Limited Warranty and which is returned to Microsoft with a copy of your receipt. This Limited Warranty is void if failure of the SOFTWARE or hardware has resulted from accident, abuse, or misapplication. Any replacement SOFTWARE or hardware will be warranted for the remainder of the original warranty period or thirty (30) days, whichever is longer. Outside the United States, these remedies are not available without proof of purchase from an authorized non-U.S. source.

NO OTHER WARRANTIES. Microsoft and its suppliers disclaim all other warranties, either express or implied, including, but not limited to implied warranties of merchantability and fitness for a particular purpose, with regard to the SOFTWARE, the accompanying written materials, and any accompanying hardware. This limited warranty gives you specific legal rights. You may have others which vary from state/country to state/country.

NO LIABILITY FOR CONSEQUENTIAL DAMAGES. In no event shall Microsoft or its suppliers be liable for any damages whatsoever (including without limitation, damages for loss of business profits, business interruption, loss of business information, or any other pecuniary loss) arising out of the use of or inability to use this Microsoft product, even if Microsoft has been advised of the possibility of such damages. Because some states/countries do not allow the exclusion or limitation of liability for consequential or incidental damages, the above limitation may not apply to you.

U.S. GOVERNMENT RESTRICTED RIGHTS

The SOFTWARE and documentation are provided with RESTRICTED RIGHTS. Use, duplication, or disclosure by the Government is subject to restrictions as set forth in subparagraph (c)(1)(ii) of The Rights in Technical Data and Computer Software clause at DFARS 252.227-7013 or subparagraphs (c)(1) and (2) of the Commercial Computer Software — Restricted Rights 48 CFR 52.227-19, as applicable. Manufacturer is Microsoft Corporation, One Microsoft Way, Redmond, WA 98052-6399.

This Agreement is governed by the laws of the State of Washington.

Should you have any questions concerning this Agreement, or if you desire to contact Microsoft for any reason, please write: Microsoft Sales and Service, One Microsoft Way, Redmond, WA 98052-6399.

CORPORATE ORDERS

If you're placing a large-volume corporate order for additional copies of this *Step by Step* title, or for any other Microsoft Press title, you may be eligible for our corporate discount.

Call **1-800-888-3303, ext. 63460,** for details.

5.25-inch Practice File disk for *Microsoft FoxPro® for Windows™ Step by Step*

You can order the enclosed Practice File disk in 5.25-inch format—free of charge. Include only shipping charges of $5.00 per disk. To order, request item number **097-000-852**. Send your name and address (no P.O. Boxes please), and daytime phone number along with your check or money order for shipping (U.S. funds only) to: Microsoft Press, Attn: FoxPro SBS disk, One Microsoft Way, Redmond, WA 98052-6399. Allow 2–3 weeks for delivery. Offer valid in the U.S. only.